Smart
Thinking

Acknowledgements

Thanks to Random House for permission to cite
Dr Susan Jeffers (*Feel the Fear . . . And Beyond*, Susan
Jeffers, Rider Books, 1998).

Thanks to Norma Black for permission to cite her
excellent school resource 'Creating A Confident School'
(*The Learning Game*, 1998).

And many thanks to Brenda and Jude at Piccadilly
Press for their vision, invaluable suggestions and
encouragement.

Frank McGinty *lives near Glasgow with his wife and family. Following his degree in literature and psychology he became a secondary school teacher. He now works as Principal Guidance Teacher at a Glasgow comprehensive, and regularly gives talks and seminars on accelerated learning, confidence-building, and achievement strategies. This is his first book.*

Smart Thinking

– Confidence and Success Sorted!

Frank McGinty

Piccadilly Press • London

*To my wife, Grace, who always inspires me
with her love and enthusiasm for life!*

First published in Great Britain in 2001
by Piccadilly Press Ltd.,
5 Castle Road, London NW1 8PR

Text copyright © Frank McGinty, 2001
All rights reserved. No part of this publication may be
reproduced, stored in a retrieval system, or transmitted in any
form or by any means, electronic, mechanical, photocopying,
recording or otherwise, without the prior
permission of the copyright owner.

The right of Frank McGinty to be identified as Author of this work
has been asserted by him in accordance with the Copyright,
Designs and Patents Act 1988

A catalogue record for this book is available from
the British Library

ISBNs: 1 85340 745 3 (trade paperback)
1 85340 750 X (hardback)

1 3 5 7 9 10 8 6 4 2

Printed and bound in Great Britain
by Bookmarque Ltd.

Cover design by Fielding Design Ltd.
Design by Judith Robertson

Set in 10pt Chianti

Contents

Introduction	**Be More!**	6
Chapter 1	**It's All About Belief**	8
Chapter 2	**Confidence, Belief . . . And Something Called Suggestibility!**	16
Chapter 3	**More About Positive Language**	27
Chapter 4	**Confidence Is Transferable!**	37
Chapter 5	**We Have Nothing To Fear But Fear Itself**	49
Chapter 6	**Use Your Brains!**	58
Chapter 7	**Confidence-building – With Attitude!**	68
Chapter 8	**Setting Goals**	81
Chapter 9	**Live Your Dreams**	95
Chapter 10	**Assertiveness Rules!**	104
Chapter 11	**Half-empty Or Half-full?**	111
Chapter 12	**Take A Break!**	119
Chapter 13	**And Finally!**	124

Introduction

Be More!

With smart thinking you don't need to settle for less. You can learn to be more. More what, did you ask?

Well, how about . . . ?

✓ More Able

✓ More Achieving

✓ More Assertive

✓ More Caring

✓ More Confident

✓ More Contented

✓ More Creative

- ✓ More Dynamic
- ✓ More Energetic
- ✓ More Expressive
- ✓ More Fulfilled
- ✓ More Fun-loving
- ✓ More Giving
- ✓ More Positive
- ✓ More Sensitive
- ✓ More Skilful
- ✓ More Studious
- ✓ More Supportive

Interested? Read on . . .

Chapter 1

It's All About Belief

*'If you think you can, you can.
If you think you can't, you're right.'*

Henry Ford

Whether they are football fans or not, most people will probably remember the year Sir Alex Ferguson successfully led Manchester United to win 'The Treble' – the two main competitions in England plus the European Champions' Cup. Many football commentators had said it was impossible. After all, it had never been done in the history of the game. But United did it . . . Millions around the world watched on TV as Sir Alex and The Reds arrived back in Manchester as Champions of Europe. As the team walked into a massive covered arena, there was an almighty roar. Sir Alex beamed like a doting grandfather. His gaze swept around the arena and suddenly something seemed to grab his attention. He smiled, gave a thumbs-up sign, and the TV camera obligingly zoomed in on the detail. It was a banner which in bold letters said:

IT'S ALL ABOUT BELIEF

Sir Alex had risen from humble beginnings to become one of the greatest football coaches of all time.

What made him different? What singled him out from thousands of others? Was it simply a matter of talent?

Probably not! If you read Sir Alex's biography you're bound to be impressed by two things:

1 He **believed** in himself.
2 He took **action** to reach his goals.

That's what this book is about. It shows you how to:

BELIEVE IN YOURSELF.

SET TARGETS.

TAKE ACTION TO REACH THOSE TARGETS.

But haven't teenagers more than enough belief in themselves? The children of the twenty-first century are bursting with confidence. They're not like their parents and grandparents when they were young . . .

This is what some sections of the media would have us believe. But recent research tells us – and many of you will know this from your own experience – that the stress and anxiety levels of teenagers are at an all-time high.

Pressure

Many young people are at breaking point with the pressures that are placed on their shoulders:

- pressure to be 'cool';
- pressure to work;
- pressure to succeed at school;
- pressure to get that place at college;
- pressure to get that job;
- pressure from parents;
- pressure from teachers.

Achieve! Succeed! Work harder! How often have you come home from school and flopped down like a wet homing-pigeon – tired, exhausted, on the edge of collapse?

Or maybe that's not your response. Maybe you don't push yourself, demonstrating to the world at large that you don't care, that you're not going to play along with know-all teachers and parents. You may successfully avoid the pressure, but what happens to your self-esteem and confidence? What happens later when the recriminations set in: the inferiority feelings, the knowledge that you could have made more of yourself, the feeling of being trapped in a dead-end . . . and possibly heading for a downward spiral into depression?

IT'S ALL ABOUT **BELIEF**

It may sound unlikely, but both of these reactions can stem from the same source: **fear**. If it goes unchecked fear can worm its way into all our lives, affecting our achievements, our successes, and our happiness.

➤ Fear of failure can drive people to work furiously – but they live in anxiety, unable to relax or enjoy their success, and everything they achieve is at a tremendous cost to themselves.
➤ Fear of failure can hold us back, so that we never fully go for it, and never reach our potential.
➤ Fear of failure can also mean that we don't try, but pretend that we aren't interested – if you don't try, you can't fail!

There are always exceptions to these: some people sail through life without a care. They enjoy success at different levels without any of the crippling doubts that others suffer. Other people are just lazy or disinterested – success and achievement don't matter to them. However, most of us fall somewhere in the three categories above. We fear because we lack **belief** in our abilities. What a pity! If we only realised how much we are capable of.

Take a few moments to think about the most fantastic organ in the human body . . .

The Brain

People who study the brain used to think that in the course of a lifetime the average person would use no more than two per cent of their brain's potential. Modern research now suggests that this is way off the mark. It would seem that we use less than one per cent! Ordinary people (that's you, me and everyone else!) are endowed with brain cells in abundance. There's some argument about exactly how many, but we know that we each have BILLIONS! *And most of these will never be used.*

Albert Einstein was one of the greatest geniuses who ever lived. He used many more brain cells than the average person, yet even he used only around ten per cent. We know this because scientists have carried out microscopic studies on his brain which, after his death, was donated for research. (They still have it pickled in a jar, somewhere in Switzerland!)

Potential Power

So if we all have such potential power why are we not using it?

Maybe it's rooted in our modern culture. You find yourself under pressure from the media to look good, to be a certain size and shape, to wear the right clothes and to be 'cool'. The group you hang around with either boasts about success and you feel pressured to keep up – or they don't value success at all, and you don't want to be ridiculed or left out. Maybe this is why so many schools are concerned about the lack of achievement among boys. Very often it's not considered 'cool' to study.

IT'S ALL ABOUT **BELIEF**

Yet there is so much concern about success.

Some of you may have parents who missed out on education and who wish to bask in the reflected glory of their children's success. Some parents are concerned about their children's future in a society that's so dependent on money. Some just have a desire for their children to do well.

Then there are parents who couldn't care less about education. You yourself may be following in their footsteps, but make no mistake about it – like everyone else, you have a vast potential just waiting to be tapped.

That's all very well. I *know* it's all about belief, but that's easier said than done. I've tried to believe in myself and got nowhere fast.

Many adults will just tell you to pull yourself together and start believing in yourself, but it's not that simple. There are ways and means of developing belief, but it seems they are not widely known.

If you'd had the life I've had, you wouldn't believe in yourself either.

Many, many young people have come up with that excuse, but by following the principles outlined in this book they have developed a spark of belief, fanned it into a flame, then really taken off.

How did they do it? Well, read on. In the following chapters you'll be given some insights into the nature of confidence and belief, then some tools to help you take the action that will change your life for the better.

SMART TIPS

1 Acknowledge feelings of fear.

2 Overcome these by learning to believe in yourself.

3 Set targets.

4 Take action to reach these targets.

Chapter 2

Confidence, Belief . . . And Something Called Suggestibility!

Lisa's Story

Lisa studies music at secondary school, specialising in piano and keyboards. She's an excellent player, but she readily admits that she hasn't always found it easy:

I used to get so uptight. Sometimes a piece would have a tricky bit and I would tie my fingers in knots trying to play it. The more I tried, the more I convinced myself I would never get it. Many a time I felt like picking the keyboard up and smashing it through the window!

But now I have a simple routine that I go through every time before I start playing, and it's made all the difference . . .

The routine is one that Lisa learned from her music teacher who also teaches personal and social education (PSE). Her teacher takes up the story:

CONFIDENCE, BELIEF . . . & SOMETHING CALLED **SUGGESTIBILITY!**

*One day in music I noticed Lisa huffing and puffing, and becoming more and more frustrated with her playing. When I went over to help I also noticed the veins bulging on her forehead and the steam coming out of her ears! She started whingeing on about the music – an exam piece – saying things like, 'I just can't play this. It's too hard.' The solution was obvious. I asked Lisa to step outside the room with me, and I reminded her – rather sharply, I must say! – of some of the things we had been discussing in PSE, but which she was obviously forgetting. When she returned to her keyboard five minutes later, she put these into practice, and **within minutes** she had worked out the fingering and phrasing for the bits she'd been finding 'impossible'. At the end of the lesson she had a big smile on her face; the piece had been well and truly mastered . . .*

So what had been going on in PSE?

The class had been learning about intelligence, attitude and achievement. Heavy stuff, but hang in there! A lot of recent research seems to indicate that whether or not you succeed in school will depend not so much on how 'brainy' you are – we've all got billions of untapped brain cells, remember – but on how positive your attitude is. Lisa's class had been using a course called 'Creating a Confident School' which taught that when you constantly focus on negative things, you get negative results.

If you keep saying 'I can't' 'This is too hard' and 'I'm stuck!' then you're absolutely right and you'll get nowhere. Keep it up and before long you'll become one of those people who home in on faults, no matter how trivial, and overlook the good points in any situation.

Positive Language

On the other hand, if you keep using positive language and focus on the good points, you'll be amazed at the results. This is what Lisa had been overlooking in music. Her negative language was pulling her down. Outside the classroom the teacher took her through a simple breathing routine to calm her down, then Lisa repeated over and over:

'I can learn the piece.'
'I have more than enough talent to succeed.'

Yes, it was a challenge, but she was up to it, she told herself. Back in class she took it slowly, calmly, positively and – *bingo!* – within minutes she was on her way.

Negative attitudes can literally destroy lives, yet they can be so deeply embedded in the subconscious mind that shifting them can be a daunting task. Before looking at some of the techniques for removing them once and for all, it's important to see how they got there in the first place.

CONFIDENCE, BELIEF . . . & SOMETHING CALLED SUGGESTIBILITY!

The Subconscious
What do the human mind and an iceberg have in common?

No matter how massive an iceberg may appear, the bad news for the ship approaching it is that only the tip is showing above the water, and about nine-tenths are spread out below. The conscious mind is like the tip of the iceberg; there's a whole lot more going on in the subconscious mind, under the surface. That's where all the memories and associations are stored. When new information is presented to the brain, it has to be filtered through a whole maze of previous experiences: likes, dislikes, impressions, fears, prejudices and so on. It's as if, whenever you're being presented with new information, you say to yourself, 'What am I to make of this?' Part of the brain then says, 'Well, here's what you felt (or thought) the last time there was something similar. This might help you decide.' And so patterns or habits are formed in the mind.

Now these habits can be positive or negative, helpful or unhelpful. If you were terrified by a dog when you were a child, you could spend your whole life being uneasy with dogs. On the other hand, you'll have noticed how some people are always delighted to see dogs. They reach out to them, fondling and stroking them without any hint of anxiety. No prizes for guessing what *their* previous experiences were!

Suggestibility

At certain times the human mind is very *suggestible*. This means that there are times when information goes straight into the subconscious mind and takes root, as it were. There's no resistance, no questions asked. The information stays there undisturbed, often creating havoc, even for a lifetime.

Your mind is in a suggestible state when you're very relaxed and calm. Funnily enough it can also be highly suggestible when you're agitated and confused. But possibly the most suggestible time of all is childhood. That's when many of our deep-seated attitudes are formed. A child's self-image is formed by the feedback (s)he gets from life, and this view is carried forward into adulthood.

A multi-millionaire business tycoon puts his success down to the fact that when he was a boy his mother always told him to be on the lookout for the person who was going to be *second* best. The implication being that in every situation he was going to be the best!

Tom's Story

For much of his life Tom was under the impression that he couldn't count. The world of mathematics was a mystery to him. Fortunately his main interests in life were language and music, so he was able to get by without too much embarrassment. But it was different when he was a teenager. His dad had a small grocer's shop and Tom and his brothers

CONFIDENCE, BELIEF . . . & SOMETHING CALLED **SUGGESTIBILITY!**

were expected to help out. Fair enough, only Tom stubbornly refused to serve the customers. This caused endless fights, as his dad thought he was just being selfish or lazy, or both. The truth, of course, was that Tom just couldn't handle money. They had no computerised tills, and all calculations had to be done in the head or on paper! For many years after that Tom thought he was disabled in some way. When God was giving out mathematical skills, he had missed Tom out . . .

It can all be traced back, though, to childhood events when Tom's mind was in a *suggestible* state. Now a grown man, Tom recalls the events:

In my early years I was taught by a teacher who could perhaps have been more patient with her class. I remember I used to enjoy working with 'sums' as we called them, and I would work away at my own pace. Unfortunately, this wasn't the teacher's pace and she yelled at me constantly. 'Hurry up, you're as slow as a snail! How much longer do we have to wait?'

I came to dread the mental arithmetic sessions when she would hover round the room like a witch on her broomstick and pounce on her prey. She would rattle off an enormous list of figures and expect an instant answer. Needless to say, she never got one from me. My brain would go into panic mode, and that was that!

Tom eventually moved on to secondary school. He could be forgiven for thinking his problems were over. But no!

There in the maths department, as if waiting just for me, was the King of Ridicule, the Master of the Put-down himself. This teacher used to separate the class into two groups, the Mathematicians and the Stupid People. You can guess which group I was in! Many a time he and the 'bright' ones would sit back and laugh as we Stupid People hung our heads and struggled with equations.

So when I left school I had no qualification in maths; instead, I had the certainty that I was unintelligent in that subject. It never occurred to me that sheer bad teaching might have had something to do with it.

Later, using the techniques outlined in this book, Tom was able to start from scratch and learn all the maths he should have learned before. He's discovered that he's actually *good* at maths; *but then, like you, he always was!*

Self-image

The point is that our self-image is largely formed by the feedback we get from others. If you have been damaged by the destructive comments or behaviour of others, then gaining this awareness is the first step in putting things right. Being bitter or resentful only makes matters worse. Recognise that we are all 'victims of victims'. Tom, for example, no longer

CONFIDENCE, BELIEF . . . & SOMETHING CALLED SUGGESTIBILITY!

thinks of his teachers as *bad* people. He's sure they never realised or intended the harm they did. They were just unenlightened or badly trained or whatever.

Luke's Story

Luke is a magician who performs at top cabarets and functions all over the country. Although successful and very busy, Luke devotes some of his time to schools, giving motivational talks to students. His talks are cleverly laced with astonishing magic tricks. But even more amazing is Luke's story.

A loser turned winner

At school Luke was a classic non-achiever. He was bullied, ridiculed and left school with no qualifications and no job prospects. Eventually he began to hit the bottle – hard! His school experiences had left him with no self-esteem. Fortunately his girlfriend talked him into attending a course in 'positive thinking'. Luke felt that this had nothing to offer him, but he went along anyway. And listened!

He heard the speaker say that if you really wanted something in life, all you had to do was keep **visualising** it and take the action that would present itself. You had to see yourself in that situation *as if it were happening now*. This angered Luke! It all sounded so easy, and he knew life was anything but.

At the end of the talk he made a point of staying behind to confront the speaker. What could he, Luke, do as he was good at nothing? 'There must be *something*,' said the speaker, 'something that you would really like to do. Admit to yourself what it is. If you feel drawn to it, that's a sure sign you'll be good at it.'

There *was* something; Luke had always been fascinated by magic tricks. But he couldn't possibly be good at that, could he?

He plucked up the courage to go along to a bookshop to see what they had about magic. All they had was a book on card tricks. Luke was disappointed, but he bought the book nevertheless *and* treated himself to a brand new pack of cards. At home he opened the book at page one. He tried to shuffle his new cards – and they ended up in a heap on the floor! Luke felt down, but he stuck at it. He was out of work, so he had plenty of time on his hands after all. He remembered the words of the course leader. And he practised. And practised. And practised . . .

The rest, as they say, is history. Luke *developed* self-belief and took the necessary action to achieve his goal. Now he is very much in demand and has found happiness. He does his voluntary work in schools as he is conscious of the vast amount of teenagers whose lives come to nothing. He knows he could so easily have been one of them.

It doesn't matter what talents you have. But rest assured

CONFIDENCE, BELIEF . . . & SOMETHING CALLED **SUGGESTIBILITY!**

you have many! If you believe you have none, or if you have yet to become confident about them, then you are a victim of negative suggestions, just as Lisa, Tom and Luke were in their different ways. It's time for change!

> ## SMART TIPS
>
> *1 Think positively* – a positive attitude will help create positive results.
>
> *2 If you think you can't do or be something, step back and look at why you think this. Approach it differently – and positively – and you'll make the breakthrough!*
>
> *3 Visualise yourself getting what you want or where you want to be. Keep your goal in your head and work towards it. This increase in focus and energy will make you far more likely to achieve it.*

Chapter 3

More About Positive Language

Many people consider Muhammad Ali to be the best boxer of all time. Even those who disagree with professional boxing remember him for his positive attitude. Ask anyone who remembers Ali and they will tell you he drove the world to distraction with his cries of:

'I am the greatest! I am the greatest!'

He *talked* himself into a frame of mind, and that sustained and motivated him through the gruelling years of training and boxing that took him to the top. There was no room for self-doubt; he simply did not entertain negative thoughts for one second.

Now, no one is suggesting that you adopt Ali's manner. Many people considered him loud, arrogant and offensive. But regardless of his *manner*, there's no doubt that his technique was highly effective.

Watch Your Language!

If you're serious about succeeding in school *and* in life, the need to watch your language can't be stressed too highly. No, this isn't about using swear-words! It's about the relationship between language and attitude. Positive results depend on a positive attitude. A positive attitude is developed by positive thoughts, and positive thoughts are influenced by the words we use. Two case studies will illustrate this.

Case Study 1: The Youth Club Trips

A youth leader recalls two trips he organised, both involving travel by coach and ferry:

I think back on the first trip as the trip from hell! As soon as the coach drove off, the moaning and groaning started: the music was too loud, then it wasn't loud enough; the coach was too hot and stuffy, then it was too cold; there wasn't enough legroom between the seats; 'How long till we get there?' The moaning went on and on. Then the kids even started squabbling among themselves.

If I'd known then what I know now I would have nipped it in the bud straight away. I've long since put it down to experience, but from that point on everything started to go wrong. The driver took a wrong turning and lost his way. He hit a kerb and burst a tyre. Thanks to the

MORE ABOUT **POSTIVE LANGUAGE**

delay we missed the cross-Channel ferry and had to wait for hours.

The weather during the trip was brilliant, but the moaning continued, and things just kept going wrong. I was never so glad to get back home in my life.

I'm not saying that the negative language somehow put a bad spell on the trip! But it did influence things. The driver, for example, could have been in a better mood throughout. He was obviously niggled by all the complaints, so it's highly likely that his concentration was affected.

Can words really have such an influence on our attitudes? Quite recently the same leader was running another trip, this time to Holland. The young people had had the benefits of 'positive language' training and were well coached! The trip leader continues:

The weather forecast for the week was none too promising, but one girl got us all into the right mood by announcing that no matter what the weather, she was going to have a great time.

*Well, the weather forecasters got it wrong. It wasn't **dull**, as they'd predicted. It was windy, with dark clouds and heavy rain almost non-stop! The North Sea heaved on the overnight crossing and most of us were seasick. Yet despite all that, we had a great trip, and at the end many said it had been the best holiday of their lives.*

Positive language creates positive attitudes. Just ask any advertising agency. They spend millions each year making sure that the words and slogans in their ads are effective. Language specialists and psychologists are employed to come up with words the public will hardly even notice, but which slip into the subconscious and form favourable attitudes to the product.

Case Study 2: Flair for Fashion

A school project seemed doomed to failure until the whole thing was turned around when everyone agreed to change *one simple word*. It was a fund-raising venture. Two girls had volunteered to spend their summer helping to build schools in remote villages. One went to Africa, the other India. The girls had to raise not only the cost of their return flights, but also their living expenses and they had to contribute a certain amount to the cost of building materials. They came up with a number of fund-raising activities themselves, both in school and in the local community, and their friends decided that they wanted to help too.

As theirs was a girls' school, a fashion show was a popular choice and they came up with the title Flair for Fashion. As expected, the girls threw themselves into the project with endless enthusiasm. This was going to be the fashion show of the century! However, it wasn't long before problems raised their ugly heads. Gradually morale was eroded.

MORE ABOUT **POSTIVE LANGUAGE**

- A number of the girls who had volunteered to be models got cold feet. They would do any other job, 'As long as I don't have to go on the catwalk.'
- A major store was lending them costumes and the girls had gone to be fitted out, but later a shop assistant sold the costumes by mistake.
- Arrangements for borrowing a catwalk had fallen through.
- A replacement catwalk was eventually found but part of the structure was missing, and it couldn't be fixed properly to the front of the stage.
- The sound system was showing its age and was unreliable.
- The assembly hall doubled as an exam hall, and as exams were in progress at that time it meant that rehearsals for the show were severely curtailed.
- The scenery painters, too, couldn't get access to the hall as often as they felt they needed.

And so it went on. Problems, problems, problems! Every time there was a meeting there was one catalogue of disasters after another. Until they decided to change their language! The word

PROBLEM

was written in large letters on a flipchart, then scored through. It was agreed that in future this word would be deleted from everyone's vocabulary and would be replaced by the word

CHALLENGE.

What's the difference? Well, it's all to do with *association*. In normal everyday language a problem is something undesirable, something we'd rather not have. A challenge, on the other hand (to the confident person at least), is something stimulating, something to get your teeth into and overcome. And the subconscious, as we saw earlier, responds to the instructions it's given. 'A problem?' it seems to say. 'Right, leave it to me. I'll fill your life with all kinds of unpleasant things to make you withdraw from it!' But how does the subconscious respond when we send it something we associate with creativity? 'Oh, it's a *challenge*. Now that's different . . .'

This, of course, is a huge simplification, but the principle that the mind responds to the type of language we give it is well documented.

So what do you think happened when the 'problems' were changed to 'challenges'? Diane, one of the girls involved, can tell you:

The change in morale was amazing. The 'problems' didn't go away, but the general attitude to them changed.

MORE ABOUT **POSTIVE LANGUAGE**

> *The 'problem' of someone selling off the costumes from the first store was turned into the 'challenge' of searching further afield and coming up with something even better. Phone calls were made and letters were sent out to other stores and we actually gathered a larger and more varied selection of costumes than we had planned: there was leisurewear, sportswear, haute couture, Asian and Oriental styles, the latest teenage fashions and evening gowns . . . You name it, we got it!*
>
> *It was the same with the catwalk. It so happened that a carpenter was in school at the time doing some maintenance. A few of us approached her and asked if she could help. In no time at all a small bridging platform was made which safely secured the catwalk to the front of the stage.*

What about the 'problem' of the sound system? The sound system couldn't be fixed on time, so the girls in charge saw it as their 'challenge' to find a new one. Enquiries were made and the head of the drama department came to the rescue. She had recently bought a brand new system for her Attic Theatre which was in an annexe away from the main school building. The girls had to lug the heavy equipment up a steep hill, but this was NO PROBLEM!

And the lack of rehearsal time because of the exams? It was a case of staying behind after school, moving tables and chairs to the side, rigging up the catwalk, then dismantling it all again at the end. It was tiring and time-consuming, but the new light-hearted approach to 'challenges' seemed to make it a lot easier.

If only you could have seen that stage on opening night! The sound system was state-of-the-art, the catwalk was ideal, the costumes were spectacular, and the scenery was brilliant. But what of the models? They had been in short supply, remember. The PSE teacher in charge reached for the copy of 'Creating A Confident School' and after doing some of the confidence-building exercises (known as Brainshakers) there were so many volunteers that lots had to be drawn for the final troupe.

Nothing ventured, nothing gained. Some of the girls approached one of the leading hair salons in the country, Vidal Sassoon, and asked if they would care to do the models' hair. No problem! On the afternoon before the show a team of hairdressers arrived and worked a minor miracle. They spent hours giving almost forty girls hairstyles to enhance the costumes that they would be wearing.

That evening the show got under way. The hairdressers had intended to stay only for the beginning, but they were so captivated they couldn't bring themselves to leave. The manager of Vidal Sassoon said that in her line of work she had seen many a professional fashion show – and this one was up there with the best of them. The music, choreography,

MORE ABOUT **POSTIVE LANGUAGE**

lighting, costumes and sheer enthusiasm all blended together to create a night to remember.

The last word goes to Diane:

I often wonder what would have happened if we'd continued as we'd started – and kept thinking of our 'problems'!

> **SMART TIPS**
>
> *1 Keep your language positive – it reflects and affects your thoughts and consequently your actions.*
>
> *2 Don't think 'problem', think 'challenge'. Enjoy the challenge.*

Chapter 4

Confidence Is Transferable!

The fact that *confidence is transferable* was evident in the days after Flair for Fashion. Four girls who had not applied for university (because they thought they weren't good enough) submitted late applications and all four were accepted. They've been in touch since they left school, and all four are happily settled in their new courses. One of them put it this way:

*I never thought in a thousand years I could be a model on a catwalk. But I was . . . So I wondered what other 'impossible' things I could do. Why **couldn't** I go to university? I'd got the grades, after all.*

She had the ability. All she lacked was the self-belief. And by taking part in the fashion show she had stepped out of her **Comfort Zone** and taken a risk – a risk that paid off handsomely.

Comfort Zones

Let's examine this idea more closely. You are said to be in your 'Comfort Zone' when you are completely comfortable and familiar with everything around you: your job, your school, your friends, your neighbourhood, your leisure activities, your *lifestyle*. You may think of yourself as having many smaller Comfort Zones. For example, you may be completely at ease in your home, but going to school or to work can make you feel less comfortable or even under threat.

It would seem sensible, then, to encourage Comfort Zones. But believe it or not, if you remain in a Comfort Zone too long you're on the slippery slope to stagnation. It's probably because all that potential discussed earlier needs to be stirred! If not, it becomes stodgy and stale and brings about either a condition of nervousness and anxiety, or apathy and a lack of contentment.

So many adults who have become cynical and disillusioned with life say the same thing in different ways, but it amounts to, 'Is this all there is to life? Life is so boring.' All the hopes and dreams of their youth have come to nothing, and they think that's just the way life is. *Nothing could be further from the truth*!

Anna's Story

Anna was a young woman in her early twenties and she had an administrative job in a government office. She had left

CONFIDENCE IS TRANSFERABLE!

school with very few qualifications, but it was obvious to anyone who spoke to her that she was a highly intelligent person.

During the summer breaks from college many students used to take part-time jobs in the office, and Anna always made a point of seeking them out. She used to quiz them about student life: she wanted to know all about the lectures, the seminars, the courses, and all about the clubs and activities.

She was so keen that many of the students encouraged her to join them. Clearly she would fit in well. All she had to do was attend night-classes, gain the necessary entry qualifications and file an application for university. Any time this was suggested to her the result was the same. She would become excited at the prospect of fulfilling what was obviously her dream – then her face would flush, her brow would furrow, and she would come up with excuse after excuse:

> *It would mean giving up my job.*
> *What if it didn't work out?*
> *What if I found the courses too difficult?*
> *What if I couldn't make ends meet?*
> *What if I had to give up my car?*

What if . . . What if . . . She always came up with some reason to stop her taking the action that would lead to the life she longed for. You see, up to a point she was content. She had a secure job. Financially she was not well-off, but she was comfortable, with a guaranteed pay cheque every month. She got on well with her colleagues and she knew her job inside out. *She was safe and warm in her Comfort Zone.*

So why change things? The answer was simple. She was becoming bored to the point of rigidity doing the same undemanding tasks day after day. Anna was capable of much more and she knew it. But the drives to keep her inside her Comfort Zone were strong and powerful, and overcame her desire for change. Years later the word was that Anna was still in the same office, still talking about change but never making the move. Maybe some day she will, and will save herself from the fate so many people in her position suffer: a downward spiral into self-loathing and frustration.

Now, this is not to suggest that everyone doing undemanding or semi-skilled jobs is doomed. Many people enjoy this type of work and find their fulfilment elsewhere. The challenge arises when people are *not* satisfied.

Push Back Those Limits!

Look at the diagram on the next page and you'll see there's usually one dominant and very powerful emotion behind all the drives to keep you in your Comfort Zone.

CONFIDENCE IS TRANSFERABLE!

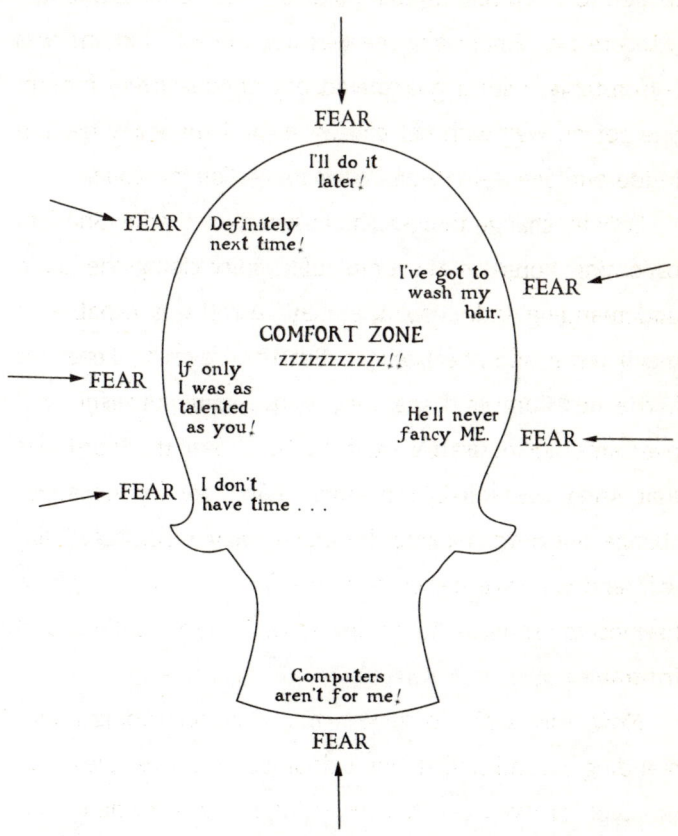

Fear comes in many disguises, but when you scrape below the surface you can usually see it for what it is.

How about **procrastination**, or as some wise person called it, 'the thief of time'? It means putting off until tomorrow what can be done today. We all tend to do exactly that with something we find challenging. 'I'll do it

SMART THINKING

tomorrow, or at the weekend.' Or, 'I'll wait till after the holiday, I'll have more energy then.' Or how about, 'I'm just not ready yet; I'll work on it.' But all too often it never gets done. Not because we haven't the time or energy, but because deep down we're afraid to take on the challenge.

What about underestimating our abilities? This is a very common problem that keeps people in their Comfort Zones. Any teacher will tell you about boys and girls who don't contribute to discussions, or who don't take part in plays and concerts, or who won't stand up to give a speech – all because they think they don't have the ability. But all the time there's an underlying fear of making fools of themselves and this keeps them firmly rooted in their comfortable, non-threatening routines.

How about health excuses? Listen to this teacher whose life was changed by overcoming a fear of rollercoasters!

I always enjoyed school trips but any time we went to a theme park I wouldn't go near a rollercoaster. I thought I would have a heart attack. Complete nonsense! Eventually I realised it was nothing but good, old-fashioned fear that was holding me back. And now that I've overcome this fear there's no stopping me. Oblivion and Nemesis at Alton Towers? Let me at them!

But how did this change come about?

CONFIDENCE IS TRANSFERABLE!

I was helped by the example of our school chaplain, Sister Maria, a nun who used to come on all our trips. Sister Maria was the oldest in the group, but she was always the first in line at every ride and she positively shrieked with laughter!

It's all to do with attitude, and remember, confidence is transferable. Here's the pay-off:

Overcoming my health fear on rollercoasters has helped me overcome a fear of flying. Now flying is one of the main pleasures in my life and it opens up so many travel opportunities.

Overcoming your fear in one area can give you the courage to push back the limits of your Comfort Zone in another. So where do you start? As a general rule you would be encouraged to 'think big' but this is an exception. Tackle small challenges that enable you to press at the limits of your Comfort Zone, then you'll develop the confidence to take on the bigger ones that will push back the boundaries. You then create a new, expanded Comfort Zone and this improves the quality of your life. In time you push the limits even further and your sense of achievement and *contentment* increases. If this becomes a life-long process you'll always have new interests, you'll always find life exciting and fear will be kept well and truly in its place.

Because fear will never leave you.

It's part of human nature, but it doesn't have to dominate and control. *You* can control it.

Excitement

Notice again the effect that language can have. What would happen if we deleted the word 'fear' and replaced it with something more encouraging? It's important that feelings aren't *denied*, but there's nothing to stop them being given other names. Everyone is familiar with the stomach-churning anxiety that the teacher on the rollercoaster must have felt, but if instead we got into the habit of calling it 'excitement' or a 'sensation associated with development', we'd already be halfway through that barrier.

So start with the small things. Maybe you often know the answer to a question in class, but you feel you would die if you answered aloud. You won't!

Push back those limits!

Maybe in class discussions you take a back seat and leave the talking to others. Have a go, chip in.

Push back those limits!

Maybe you're a great musician, but no one's ever heard you play. Before you perform at a concert or assembly, you

CONFIDENCE IS TRANSFERABLE!

could get used to practising in a more open place. Let people hear you.

Push back those limits!

Maybe you'd like to enter a competition, but never quite get your name in. Do it now.

Push back those limits!

Lee's Story

A student who really impressed everyone with her sheer courage was a girl called Lee Divers. In her early years at school Lee was a shy, retiring girl whose confidence could have been a whole lot better. At parents' evenings Lee's teachers always said that she had to work on her confidence; she was a bright girl, but needed to believe in herself; she should speak out more . . . you know the sort of things teachers say. Lee took this to heart and soon discovered a talent in art and design. She worked and worked and her efforts paid off in exam success.

When she was in Year Twelve Lee threw herself enthusiastically into the fashion show, Flair for Fashion, which you heard about earlier. As well as designing some of the costumes, Lee was the leader of a dance group that was going to perform at the close of the show. Rehearsals were proceeding (despite all those challenges!) and the dancers were relying heavily on Lee for choreography and inspiration.

A few days before the show, however, Lee announced that she would have to withdraw as she had received an invitation to an interview at the London College of Fashion. This was a major achievement. The London College of Fashion has a great reputation and attracts applicants from all over the world. Not bad for a young girl from a part of Glasgow that doesn't always have a positive image! This was great news for Lee, but not so good for the show. Nevertheless it was accepted as just another 'challenge'.

On the day of the show, Lee came in and said that she *could* take part after all. Secretly her teacher was disappointed, as it looked as if she had pulled out of the interview. The show was on Thursday night, after all, and the interview was scheduled for early Friday morning.

That evening the show got under way. Lee's teacher recalls:

I noticed that on a few occasions Lee rather nervously asked me what time it would finish. I was curious, and when I asked her why she was asking, she apologised and said it was just that she had to catch a bus. When I asked where she was going, she was surprised and said, 'London, of course'. She then went on stage and put herself through a punishing dance routine. The audience wanted more so she and her troupe had to do it all again.

As soon as the show finished Lee had to dash for the bus station. Not for her the after-show party and celebrations!

CONFIDENCE IS TRANSFERABLE!

Instead it was a seat on the overnight bus to London. Can you picture the forlorn figure sitting nervously at the window as the bus pulled out into the darkness on its long, overnight trek? A refreshing night's sleep would be out of the question. Then, in the morning, what would it be like trying to freshen up before the interview? Drained from the show, exhausted from the journey, alone in a strange city, can you imagine pitting yourself against candidates from all over the world? How far out of your Comfort Zone can you get?

Well, was Lee successful? *Of course she was!* With her grit and determination, there was only going to be one outcome. Confidence is transferable, so it's highly likely that although physically tired, Lee would be inspired by her twofold success: success in the show itself and success in getting herself from the late-night show to the early-morning interview 650 kilometres away.

Success breeds success, so the up-beat feelings from the night before would stand her in good stead. Lee beat off many applicants and was offered one of only a few places.

When asked for permission to tell her story, Lee was delighted. She said: 'Tell them it works. I remember what I was like and look at me now.'

SMART TIPS

1 Tackle your fears. Every time you overcome them and do something you thought you couldn't do, you will become more confident.

2 Confidence is transferable – use it to tackle other new things and you'll find success comes more easily, and your confidence keeps growing.

3 Step out of that Comfort Zone. Set new challenges – however small – and you'll grow in confidence and fulfilment.

Chapter 5

We Have Nothing To Fear But Fear Itself

You've seen how fear can hold us back and keep us from taking the action we need to improve our lives. This type of fear usually comes from the steady *drip, drip, drip* of negative messages into the subconscious mind, usually during childhood or at other highly suggestible stages of our lives.

This fear can be handled, as we've just seen, by using the Comfort Zone idea and *pushing back the limits*. However, there is another, often more serious type of fear which many young people know only too well. It's called a **trauma**.

Trauma
This is the result of one or more physical or emotional shocks. We're dealing here with the emotional variety, and it's no exaggeration to say that the effects of a trauma can be devastating. A single emotional shock in childhood can

literally affect a person for life. The good news is that traumas, like other types of fear, can be completely overcome.

Most people experience these emotional shocks to some degree. Let Simon tell you about one that he has overcome.

Simon's Story

My father used to speak of his horrific experiences in the Rescue Service during World War II; he had to pick up survivors, often badly mutilated, from the Atlantic Ocean. This had a traumatic effect on him, but over the years his constant stories had the same effect on me! So I spent most of my early years in a state of terror, imagining there were monsters everywhere.

To make matters worse, when I was twelve I went to a boarding school. It was in a lovely country setting but, of course, it was haunted . . . I well remember looking at a massive portrait of the school's Victorian founder and running for my life when his eyes seemed to follow me!

There were four large dormitories, but only three were in use – something terrible was supposed to have happened in the fourth. (There was no doubt some good reason for not using it, but no one was interested in that!) Then one day I came down with rubella and had to be isolated, so where did they put me? Yes, on my own in the 'haunted' dormitory.

Needless to say, on the first night I was breathless with terror. The horrors from my dad's stories, the monsters of my childhood and now the fear of the haunted dormitory seemed to grip my heart. I expected something to happen – and eventually it did . . . At first I thought it was just the floorboards, but it had a definite rhythm. It was footsteps!

At the far end of the dorm was a large figure, shrouded in a black cloak with a hideously glowing face. Surely it was the man in the portrait, coming for his next victim? I recall the figure coming closer, closer, then . . . nothing.

I know now that I fainted. I remember coming round and the school nurse telling me my temperature was 104°F, or 40°C. The truth emerged. My housemaster had come to check that I was OK. He was wearing a black teacher's gown and in his hand he had a small flashlight. He had been walking slowly so as not to disturb me. My fears were probably heightened by my high temperature, so I interpreted his footsteps as a threat, his gown as some ghoulish garb – and his face? Well, maybe his flashlight was giving him a 'glow'. Or maybe I just imagined it. It was that kind of night!

Well, Simon survived. But don't think there were no ill-effects. His difficulties were made more intense by the fact that he told no one about this experience. He had caring

SMART THINKING

parents, teachers and friends, but he told not one person.

When a fear or shock is *repressed* (when you pretend to yourself that it never really happened) it can play havoc with your day-to-day living. So why didn't Simon confide in anyone about his fears and dreads?

For one thing, there was the embarrassment: it's not cool for boys to be afraid. There was also the sheer terror of reliving the experience. It seemed much better to try and forget it, then it might go away.

But fears that are denied do *not* go away. For Simon, that was the start of a whole series of nightmares and a dread of 'lights-out' in the dormitory. Perhaps more significantly, that was the start of a severe deterioration in both his behaviour and his schoolwork. Until then his grades had been very good indeed. Now they plummeted until they were the lowest in his class. That worked wonders for his self-esteem! So as a defence he adopted a 'See if I care!' attitude and his behaviour became an embarrassment to himself and his parents.

Simon was eventually able to rid himself of these traumas, but not before he left school with qualifications that in no way reflected his ability. His fears and anxieties were taking over his life, and it got to the stage that he either had to sink or swim! Fortunately, he gained the courage to ask for advice, then:

- by READING AND LEARNING about how the traumas were caused and how they were affecting his daily life, he was able to understand and come to terms with them;
- by TALKING AND TALKING about his experiences to mature, sympathetic listeners, he was able to face his fears and get them out of his system;
- by doing activities like the ones you'll be encouraged to do in later chapters, he was able rebuild his self-esteem and self-belief.

You've seen just how devastating the effects of a trauma can be, but now Simon's able to help others with similar troubles. Perhaps there's something in *your* background that's had a similar debilitating (or 'holding back') effect. For example:

- you may have lost a parent or other close member of your family and have yet to cope with it effectively;
- you may have witnessed domestic violence;
- you may have been abused: verbally, emotionally, physically, sexually, or all four;
- you may have had an accident or a near-miss that has terrified you;
- you may have been bullied at school or somewhere else.

Perhaps your particular trauma is more mundane and less severe in its effects, but it could be holding you back nevertheless. Some young people develop anxiety by listening to the 'prophets of doom' on the TV news, telling us we're on the brink of extinction through AIDS, threats of nuclear war, global warming or whatever.

Very often when a trauma is repressed during the early years the person forgets the incident entirely, but the fear comes out in one or more ways. A fear of needles, a fear of heights, a fear of the sight of blood, or an exaggerated fear of injury and death – all these phobias are usually the side effects of buried traumas.

There are also the other fears, discussed in Chapter Two, which are caused not so much by traumas but by early **negative suggestion**, like a fear of talking to new people or of 'letting go' and being yourself. If you've never told anyone about your fear, then you're carrying a huge burden. Keeping the lid on it all uses up lots of nervous energy. Think of all that energy going to waste: you're just sitting around reading a magazine or watching TV, yet you're 'leaking' energy. No wonder you constantly feel tired or irritable or unable to cope! Keeping the hatches firmly battened on your fears also affects your self-esteem: you feel inferior; you lack confidence; somehow you're just 'not the same' as the rest.

Now for the good news

Traumas and phobias can be tackled effectively in the following way: summon up your courage and SHARE

WE HAVE **NOTHING TO FEAR** BUT FEAR ITSELF

your thoughts and feelings, just as Simon did. Opening up to someone you trust can work wonders. It does a number of things:

1 It helps bring those fears that have been festering away in the subconscious out into the open; fears can't live in the light of exposure so they wither and die. There's a very old and wise saying: 'Face a fear and the death of that fear is certain.'

2 Talking also helps to heal the psychological havoc that fear has been creating. You soon begin to realise you've been tricked. You are the same as others and you can begin to accept yourself; you're not a wimp or a coward or a loser!

3 By sharing your fears you learn to lighten up and not take yourself too seriously.

Another thing you can do is read and learn about how the mind works. In this way you gain the KNOWLEDGE to understand yourself. Knowledge empowers you to build confidence and gain control of your life.

If all else fails, you can get professional help; this can be arranged through your doctor or your school, and a trained counsellor will gently guide you through the web of fear and confusion that's stifling you.

When the Russian leader, Lenin, was a child he had a fear

of the dark. To overcome this he used to creep out through his bedroom window after lights-out and walk in the pitch-black forest. Every step brought terror, but he clenched his teeth and got on with it. It worked.

He was later able to talk about it, but what a pity he had no one he felt he could talk to at the time. He overcame his fear the hard way, but it could have been cleared up more easily and with less danger to himself by just discussing it openly!

If you yourself are not the victim of such fears, then by reading this you might be able to help your friends. You can be the listener and just be there when you are needed.

SMART TIPS

1 Fear is sometimes the result of trauma. Talk about your fears, try to understand them and come to terms with them:

2 Having come to terms with your fears, take action to work through them and build esteem and self-belief.

Chapter 6

Use Your Brains!

There are other ways to overcome fears, and Dr Susan Jeffers has come up with an ingenious way of coping with those nagging little fears that nip away at your mind and try to stifle your self-development. Rather than ignore these fears, Dr Jeffers encourages us to talk to them! She calls the voice of fear the Chatterbox, and urges us to give our Chatterboxes a name. When you 'hear' the voice of fear – saying things like, 'Don't ask her out, she'll knock you back and you'll never live it down!' or, 'I'm going to fail this exam, I just know it!' – address it by its name and kick it out: 'Hi, So-and-so. What do you think you're doing here? Get lost!'

You can use more colourful language, but it is effective! It may seem absurd to you and maybe at this stage you wouldn't dream of trying it. But it's not as silly as it sounds. By using humour and fantasy you're drawing on *the right side of the brain*.

The Structure Of The Brain

To appreciate this you need to know a little about the structure of the brain. All the areas of the brain function as an interlinked 'whole', but it's helpful to think of three major 'compartments'.

Look at this diagram:

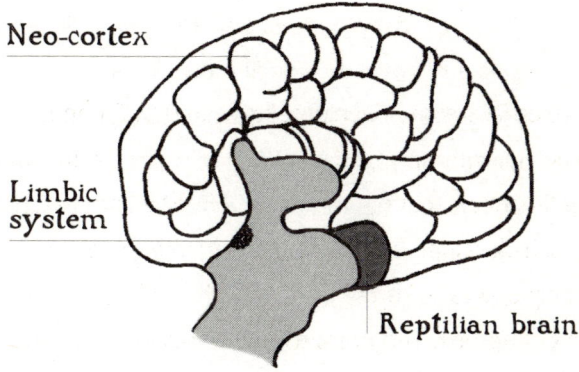

The earliest part of the brain to develop was the potato-shaped lump at the base of the skull, just above the neck. This is known as the **brain stem** or **reptilian brain** because we share it with reptiles and mammals. In the centre is the **limbic system**, and above that sits the two-sided **neo-cortex**, commonly called the 'thinking cap'.

When information comes in through the senses it's first passed through the limbic system. This is where our emotions are, and information coming in and going out is coloured with feelings. If these emotions are very strong and we feel under threat, the information is sent down to the reptilian brain. Its role is to keep bodily functions going and, when threatened, to supply the heart and arteries with blood and chemicals (such as adrenalin and cortisol) to give us the strength to run or put up a fight. Very often this means *to panic*!

This is why, when people are under stress, you often see them pacing up and down or wringing their hands – they're trying to cope with the increased flow of blood and energy. The blood needed for this increased supply is taken from the parts that don't need it right then. And the neo-cortex is one of them. In a state of panic you don't *think*, you simply *respond*.

On the other hand if you are calm and relaxed and don't allow the emotions to hold sway, the information is passed from the limbic system *upwards* to the neo-cortex where it can be processed thoughtfully and rationally. To make this happen you can consciously slow down (or sit down!) and take deeper and slower breaths. By doing this, more blood and oxygen flow into the top of the brain. The limbic system gets the message from the heart and lungs that there is no threat, so it's able to send information up to the rational neo-cortex rather than down to the unthinking reptilian brain. As a result you'll deal with your fears more calmly,

USE YOUR **BRAINS**!

openly and rationally. There are other tips for remaining calm, but first you need to know more about the neo-cortex.

The Neo-cortex

This is really two separate halves, commonly known as the Left Brain and the Right Brain, joined by a membrane called the **corpus callosum**. Look at the diagram and imagine you are looking down from above into someone's brain:

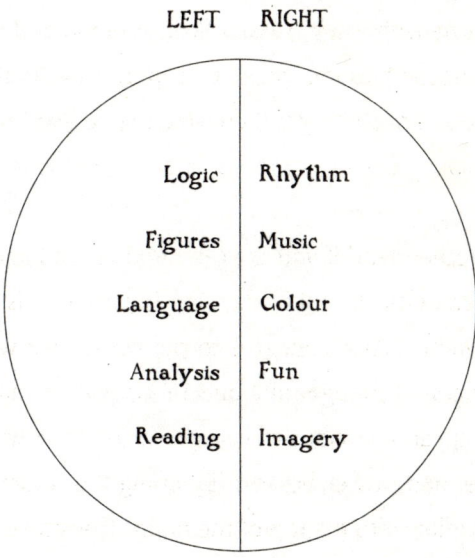

This oversimplifies the brain, but it's true to say that the Left Brain is more practical and scientific in its approach, and most of the *conscious mind* thinking comes from this side. The Right Brain deals with most of the *subconscious mind* functions and loves imagination, brightness and humour.

And these are great weapons for overcoming fear.

By *picturing* your fear as a harmless little creature perched on your shoulder that plants 'fearful' thoughts in your mind, you can then swipe it off and tell it where to go. *Laugh* at yourself in this situation and you'll relax more.

You can even develop a 'Right Brain' routine to help you deal with *external situations* that threaten you. Suppose, for example, you're about to have a discussion with a person who could be a lot more friendly and sympathetic in their approach. You want to state your case assertively, but your mouth is dry, you feel you won't be able to string your words together and you feel well and truly intimidated:

1 Take a series of slow, deep breaths.
2 Picture your fear on your shoulder and call it by its name. Smile to it and tell it to get away. Mentally brush it off; it doesn't belong here.
3 Now picture the person who intimidates you. Turn him or her into a cartoon character and reduce it in size. But don't do this in a *cruel* way; keep your pictures comical and non-threatening.
4 Now slowly and calmly state your case.

USE YOUR **BRAINS**!

Persevere! This gets a lot easier the more you practise. You can even do it with a wider audience. Last year a government 'think tank' was seeking the views of school students on a variety of issues. On the way to the venue the girl chosen to be the main speaker started panicking. She could 'see' herself drying up in front of her audience. Fortunately, she went through her routine. She *pictured* her little fear monster and laughed it off. Then a great image came to mind. She remembered a TV commercial for a car: someone was addressing an audience in a large lecture theatre, just like the one she was going to. The audience, however, was a hall full of *babies*, sitting there in their nappies, waving their rattles and gurgling and cooing at one another.

When she rose to speak that's exactly how she pictured her audience. She tells us:

As I looked around all I could see was a hall full of babies, but to make it more ridiculous they all had grown-up faces, complete with glasses, moustaches, make-up and so on. Totally non-threatening! Once I was underway with my speech and more at ease, I was able to abandon the image and relate to the audience as they really were.

Fun and laughter are great tools to have in your self-development kit. Thousands of years ago the great Chinese philosopher, Lao-tse, said:

'Being happy is the best medicine.'

So what does laughter actually do?

It creates an immediate release of tension and it causes what's known as the **sympathetic nervous system** to pump more blood up to the brain. This (as we've seen earlier) helps us think and decide more clearly. Laughter is like pressing a RESET button, so that any unnecessary 'reptilian' activity can be neutralised and you can start again. It's smart thinking to tap into the Right Brain's love of humour: the more you can laugh, the more you will deal with fear, and the more relaxed you will be. This in turn will lead to confidence and success.

Creativity

As well as helping us manage our fears, a knowledge of the Right and Left Brain functions can help us to *learn* more easily and be more *creative*. Yet, traditionally, Western education has concentrated on Left Brain activity to the neglect of the Right. We only have to think of the great geniuses of the past who were both scientific *and* artistic. Leonardo da Vinci left us great paintings as well as drawings of prototype helicopters and submarines. Einstein didn't reach his great scientific discoveries by his mathematical knowledge alone. We know that he used to sit on a hillside, go into a dream-like state, and imagine (*Right Brain activity*) that

USE YOUR **BRAINS**!

he was riding through the universe on moonbeams! Then he set about applying the mathematics.

How many days are in April? Automatically your mind is probably going through the old childhood rhyme, 'Thirty days has September, April, June and November . . .' Without this activity involving the numbers (*Left Brain*) and the rhyme (*Right Brain*) it would be much more difficult to remember which months had how many days!

Richard's Story

Richard uses this technique in his football. His skill in delivering long and accurate passes is much admired. He practises hard (*Left Brain*), but he 'visualises' too (*Right Brain*):

I noticed that when they analyse football matches on TV they often draw a computerised line between one player and another to show the path the ball will take. It makes it easier for the viewers to see how skilful the player was when he delivered the ball. When I'm playing, I imagine the same thing. Before I kick the ball I 'see' a bright red line or a looping arc between me and the other player and I just imagine the ball is stuck to it! Away it goes, and it almost always reaches its target!

There are students who take in small mascots or pictures to sit on their desks during exams. They *imagine* the mascots whispering words of encouragement, helping them to stay calm, and feeding them the answers as they write. And nobody, apart from the students themselves, knows about this – so there's no embarrassment, no ridicule, no need to explain things to others.

What goes on in your mind is your own business! So make friends with your imagination. Develop a flourishing fantasy life. *Laugh* your fears into oblivion and watch yourself take off!

USE YOUR **BRAINS**!

SMART TIPS

1 Use humour and imagination to deflate fear. Imagine the person or situation that threatens you in a funny or harmless context, reduced in size, or as a cartoon sketch!

2 Give your fear a name and a face. Talk to it. Tell it to get out of here!

3 When scared or intimidated, take deep, slow breaths and focus on calming yourself. Step away from your panic! This will help you process information through the logical, rational part of your brain and you'll deal with the situation more easily, with better results.

4 Humour and imagination help us learn and understand. Use your creativity to help you reach your goals.

Chapter 7

Confidence-building – With Attitude!

You'll realise by now that for some people taking themselves less seriously and developing self-belief will require a radical shift in attitude. No one is saying that's easy! The suggestions and other inputs that form our attitudes in the first place are so deeply embedded in the subconscious that they become a normal, unnoticed part of the brain's activity.

What exactly is an *attitude*?

An attitude is a way of viewing some person or thing, and that view is prompted by an underlying thought or feeling. Very often the thought or feeling is so deeply rooted in the subconscious that we don't even know how or when it got there. For example, someone may feel threatened by foreigners, while someone else may feel at ease with them. The reasons *why* may not be clear. They only know how they feel. An *attitude* is at work.

Culture

The culture you grow up in has an enormous effect on the formation of your attitudes.

A few years ago a teacher from California was spending an exchange year in Scotland. She was puzzled. 'This is a great country,' she would say, 'but the Scottish people I meet are always apologising for it! Why do they always think America is better?' In particular she loved the weather. Having spent most of her life in the California sun, she welcomed the chance to dress up in woolly clothes on a winter's day. She loved the rain on her face. And the students would laugh when she rushed out with her camera because she'd never before seen a blue sky with white, grey and black clouds all at the same time. Yet all she heard was people apologising for it!

We can grow up with attitudes that lead to *set beliefs* that are never questioned; some of these beliefs *sustain* us, but others can *limit* us.

The Four-minute Mile

In the early 1950s Roger Bannister was a medical student at Oxford University. He was also a keen athlete and he specialised in running the mile (approximately 1600 metres). At that time the accepted belief was that running a mile in under four minutes was *impossible*. Doctors, professors and coaches had all studied the human body and had concluded that the limits of human speed had been reached. Athletes accepted this and for years the 'four-minute barrier' stood.

But Roger Bannister did not accept it. His studies of the human body prompted him to believe that with a combination of training, diet and *attitude,* the barrier could be broken.

On 6 May 1954, at a race meeting in Oxford, history was made. Roger Bannister ran the mile in 3 minutes 59.4 seconds. The 'impossible' had been done.

But of greater interest is *what happened next*.

Within two months an Australian named John Landy established a new record of 3 minutes 58 seconds.

Within a year a new record was being set at almost every major race meeting round the world.

You see, Roger Bannister may have broken the record by an insignificant amount (0.6 of a second), but he had well and truly *shattered* the psychological barrier. Once that shift in *attitude* to the challenge had taken place, record after record was broken in a very short space of time. Now athletes are talking about running the 1500 metres in three minutes. Impossible? Let's just wait and see . . .

So we know that attitudes and beliefs can make or break the quality of our lives. Now it's time to consider another dynamic tool that will not only shift those deeply ingrained negative attitudes, but will replace them with powerful, creative ones that will help you achieve what you want.

Positive Affirmations

This activity is so simple, yet so *challenging*. The simplicity lies in the method: you only have to keep repeating short, positive statements to yourself. The challenge lies in *perseverance*, that is, keeping it going. Many people are put off by constant repetition and they give up because they find it 'boring'. To cope with that you need to be resilient: you have to *put up* with the unattractive aspects of it because you trust that there are greater rewards for you at a later stage. So before looking at the activity itself, let's look at the importance of REPETITION.

Many young people nowadays admire pop stars and footballers. They go along to a concert and are wowed by the brilliant vocals and dancing or whatever. They come away thinking it would be great to be a pop star. The glamour, the adulation, the travel, the luxury lifestyle . . . Or they go along to a football stadium and cheer as the latest hero turns on the skill. But what the public doesn't see is the hour after hour of practice, practice, practice. The striker may be revelling in the adulation of 60,000 fans and every young boy in the stadium wishes he could be him, but what they *don't* see is the sheer hard graft that the footballer has to put in, day in, day out. There's the lap after lap of the running track to improve fitness, the shot after shot at goal to improve technique. Nobody, but *nobody*, reaches the top in any field without constant practice!

Like it or not, repetition is part of learning and part of development. One of the surest ways to shift and banish negative thought patterns is to bombard the mind with positive alternatives. In recent years this process has become known as AFFIRMATION. (One of the meanings of *to affirm* is to declare something in a strong and positive manner.)

Affirmations Within Groups

The 'envelope game' is often used to introduce PSE classes to affirmations. The students have to say something nice about each other! Everybody loves this. The great American wit and novelist, Mark Twain, summed it up when he said:

'I can live for two months on a good compliment!'

Ask your teacher to try it, or you can do it in your youth club or just with a group of friends. Here's how.

Get into groups of about five. (The groups can be smaller, but then there will be fewer compliments!) The important thing is that the group members should know each other well. You will need pens, slips of paper and envelopes. A leader is appointed in each group to organise things.

CONFIDENCE-BUILDING – WITH ATTITIUDE!

1 The group leader writes the names of each member on a separate envelope and keeps the envelopes.

2 Five slips of paper are given to each member of the group (or three or four depending on how many are in the group).

3 On the first slip each person writes the name of another group member. Under the name a positive (or complimentary) comment is written. All comments must be true, accurate, sincerely felt and expressed positively, for example, 'You are really good at cheering us all up' or, 'You were a great help to me when I first came here'.

4 The process is repeated for each person on the other slips of paper. This means, of course, that each writer has to write something positive not only about the others in the group, *but about him/herself.*

5 The leader then gathers in all the comments for the first person (let's call her Susan), and the papers are put in Susan's envelope.

6 Then the comments for John (or whoever) are gathered in, and so on.

7 If this is a school activity the teacher gathers in all of the envelopes and keeps them until about five minutes before the end of the lesson. We all like to know what others think of us, so by that time the students are desperate to open their envelopes.

When the contents are read the result is always exactly the same, no matter how many groups this is done with: there is an aura of excitement, gratitude and goodwill that you can almost feel.

The Inner Child

This desire for positive feedback and reassurance from others is a basic drive in all of us. (Don't let anyone tell you it's not; they're fooling themselves!) A popular image in modern psychology, and one you may have heard of, is the 'inner child'. This suggests that deep inside each of our minds lives the small, helpless child we once were. Like all young children this one needs to be loved, reassured, encouraged and shown affection. It's very fragile and its feelings can easily be hurt, so you have to treat it very carefully and gently. Of course nobody believes that there is *literally* such a child; this is simply an *image* or *picture* of our earliest psychological needs. The feelings from that stage in our development are buried in the subconscious, but they still cry out to be heard and recognised! And very often the one who harms the Inner Child most is not someone else, but the person him/herself – the very one you would expect to be loving and caring.

This idea of nurturing, building up and caring for the inner self is what affirmations are all about. When the 'envelope game' is played in schools the reactions to the envelopes

CONFIDENCE-BUILDING — WITH ATTITIUDE!

are briefly examined during the next PSE lesson. Everyone who does this exercise gets a lift from it, so attention is now drawn to the fact that one of the comments was a *self-comment*.

If they didn't realise it before, it has become evident to everyone that praise and encouragement are very powerful boosters indeed. And this opens the door for the next step: composing personal affirmation cards.

Affirmation Cards

You too can benefit from personal affirmation cards. Buy a pack of blank postcards and get some coloured felt-tip pens. Spend some time thinking about the areas of your life that you most want to improve. You may want to rid yourself of some long-established bad habits, or you may want to develop confidence in some way (this exercise goes hand-in-hand with pushing back the limits of the Comfort Zone). You may want to improve on certain skills that you're already developing, e.g. public speaking or playing basketball! Affirmations are excellent for helping to set and reach goals (about which there will be more later).

You're now ready to compose your affirmations. To begin, select just a few areas you feel need the greatest attention. Most people believe that affirmations should be in the present rather than the future tense, but there is complete agreement that they should be *personal* and expressed only in *positive* terms. (For example, if you intend to improve your maths, say 'I now find it easier to understand maths' (*positive language*), not 'I don't get stuck at maths any more'.) You'll remember them more easily if they're short and snappy. Here are some you may wish to consider. You can make up your own along the same lines, or you can adapt these to your own circumstances, or you can just use them as they stand:

I am now a capable, confident 'A' student.
My music and drama skills are rapidly developing now.
I am now relaxed and at ease with everyone I meet.
I am open and receptive to all my school has to offer.
I am fit. I am healthy. I am grateful for my life.
I am thankful for my friends and I support them in every way.
My creativity is now developing in leaps and (knows no) bounds.
My memory is like a muscle that develops with practice.
I can study and concentrate hour after hour.
I am attracted only to substances that are good for me.
Regardless of my past, my life is now filled with positive expectations.
There is only one person in charge of my life.

Having composed or decided on your affirmations, you are now ready to copy them on to your cards. There should only

CONFIDENCE-BUILDING – WITH ATTITIUDE!

be one affirmation per card, and your lettering should be as bright and colourful as possible.

What else could you put on your cards?

Remember, the brain loves colour and *humour*. Some affirmations can verge on the serious, so if you lighten your cards up with doodles and drawings they can be more effective.

You can make several copies of your cards and pin them up in your room, on your desk, in your bathroom – or wherever you like. Some people, especially those who are working on their confidence or self-image, may be reluctant to do this in case anyone sees them, but you should consider it for three reasons:

1 Others will be naturally curious and, especially when you're getting results, you'll be happy to help them get started too. Remember, *don't take yourself too seriously*!
2 The more places you have your affirmations pinned up, the more opportunity you'll have to repeat them. (Repetition, remember, is the key to success.)
3 The more they are 'in your face' as you go about your business, the more likely they are to have a *subliminal effect*.

Those of you who do media studies will probably have heard of subliminal advertising. This is when words and/or images of products are flashed at an audience so quickly (for example, between the frames of a film) that the conscious mind misses them, but they make their way straight to the subconscious. For this reason subliminal advertising is banned in most countries, as it can influence people without them even knowing that they're being 'got at'.

In the same way, the familiar messages on your cards can be relayed to your subconscious where they will have a considerable effect. The difference now is that you have *chosen* this method; no one has forced it on you.

Being Receptive

Getting into the routine of using the affirmation cards can be a major challenge for some people. Ideally they should be used when you are relaxed and calm, as this is when your mind is most receptive. Some people find first thing in the morning and last thing at night the best times. If you're the sort of person who could be more attracted to routines, you might take more readily to the 'pin up' suggestion. And how about using a computer to produce bigger, brightly-coloured versions in a variety of styles?

Whichever method you choose, you are urged to *stick with it*. The benefits of affirmations may not be felt immediately and this puts some people off. Nowadays we're used to fast foods, instant access, and so on. As a result we tend to be less patient than we could be. This is where *resilience* comes in: if you stick with it, success is guaranteed. It's logical. Brain patterns, both positive and negative, are formed by the constant input of messages.

This is a fantastic tool for you to use in your personal development.

It can be put no stronger than that!

> ## SMART TIPS
>
> **1** Deep-rooted attitudes and beliefs can sometimes limit you. Identify them and challenge them: you can get over them.
>
> **2** Use positive affirmations: keep repeating positive statements to yourself, over and over. Persevere!
>
> **3** Write affirmation cards to yourself – using colour and humour. Keep looking at them and repeating the messages.

Chapter 8

Setting Goals

It was mentioned earlier that affirmations can be used to help you reach your goals. That's assuming you have goals. Many young people *never* set themselves targets. It's not just the apathetic students either; many of those without goals are otherwise positive, bright and committed to their development.

Think about this. In 1953 the governors of Yale University hired researchers to produce a paper on life at the university and on American life in general. A questionnaire was given to students who were leaving that year.

Question 46 asked: *Do you have goals for your life?* (Only six per cent had.)

Question 47 asked: *Have you written your goals down?* (Only four per cent had.)

In 1973 (twenty years on) the same students were interviewed again. The four per cent who had written their goals down had achieved every one of them, and appeared to be successful in all areas of their lives. But the two per cent who *had goals but had not written them down* were no better off than the other ninety-four per cent.

When you write down your goals and review them regularly, you are *affirming* your intentions. Your subconscious will see to it that you direct your life accordingly. Your subconscious, remember, does not discriminate. It simply responds to the inputs it receives.

Nelson Mandela had a goal . . .

The South African government jailed Nelson Mandela in 1962 because they didn't like his politics, which demanded equal rights for black people. He was a prisoner for twenty-seven years, often in solitary confinement and he was often tortured. During that time we know he wrote down his plans (or goals) for the future. He had a dream:

'Some day I will lead my country!'

Can you imagine what it would be like holding that dream every day and every night through the years? How would *you* feel after five years? Ten years? Fifteen years? How would you fight off depression and even despair? How could you hold a dream about leading your country when the odds were so heavily stacked against you? Yet somehow Nelson Mandela *did* hold that dream.

In February 1990, at the age of seventy-two, Nelson Mandela was released. Surely after years of confinement

SETTING **GOALS**

and often torture he would be a broken and embittered old man? Who would blame him if he retired from public life and looked for a few years of relaxation and pleasure? But that was not his style. He had a dream, a dream that had sustained him through twenty-seven years: *'Some day I will lead my country!'*

Forgiveness

He resumed the leadership of his party and in 1994 was duly elected President of the Republic of South Africa. Impressive, but what happened next was even more impressive. Many urged him to seek revenge. He had gained a position of power and could set about making life difficult for the whites who had imprisoned him. Yet with a dignity that almost defies logic he urged his people to FORGIVE. He was now the leader of the *white* people as well as the *black*, and he was determined to UNITE the races for the greater good of their country. South Africa could so easily have descended into a bloodbath, but under Mandela's leadership that catastrophe was avoided.

How was it possible for a man who had suffered so much and been robbed of so much of his life to be so forgiving?
Could it be that by constantly affirming his goals and planning success – rather than plotting revenge – his mind would

SMART THINKING

automatically steer in a positive direction, enabling him to reach the heights of dignity that the human spirit is capable of? There's no doubt about it, if you want to reach the heights of *your* capabilities, then:

- **Set goals and write them down.**
- **Affirm them regularly.**
- **Review them and amend them in the light of progress.**

When goals are mentioned to many young people they immediately think of *career* goals and this causes anxiety because they don't usually have any idea about what they want to do in their working lives. This is perfectly normal because the teenage years are a time of discovery, a time of experimentation as different ideas present themselves. Some people have a definite career path from a very early age, but most don't. How, then, can you set goals for the future?

The answer is to set goals for the most important areas of your life *as it is now*. How about the following areas?

- **Study**
- **Leisure/recreation**
- **Personal development**
- **Relationships**
- **Spiritual development**
- **Career possibilities**

Think ahead one year from the time you start planning, and divide that year into quarters. Set goals *in each category* for the three months that lie ahead and set larger goals that you want to achieve by the end of the year.

Now let's consider each category in turn.

Study
Three-monthly goals
(The following questions/suggestions might help.)
- Review your recent grades.
- Which areas need attention?
- What help do you need?
- Where will you get that help? (Teachers, books, CD-ROMs, Internet, etc.)
- Which assignments are due and when? (It's a good idea to have a school diary/planner. If your school doesn't provide one it's easy enough to buy a diary and 'customise' it for school.)
- Where is the best place to complete your assignments? (At home, in a library, at a friend's?)
- How is your attendance and timekeeping?
- Are there any other questions about your studies you can think of?

Now set your goals for the next three months.

Yearly goals

What do you intend to have achieved in your studies by this time next year?

- Improvements in specific subjects (e.g. history, biology)?
- Enrolment in a new course or courses?
- Grades to proceed to the next stage?
- Grades good enough for entry to college?
- Anything else?

Now set your overall study goals for the next year.

Leisure/Recreation
Three-monthly goals

- Review your recent leisure activities.
- Is there anything that's being given *too much* time and attention?
- Are your leisure activities out of balance with the rest of your life? (Maybe you're not giving *enough* time to them.)
- Are there any activities that are now non-productive and should be dropped?
- Are there any activities that you really want to take up, but have never had the courage to try? (Remember the Comfort Zone.)
- Is the crowd you go about with really the best one for you?
- Are there any other questions about your leisure

activities you can think of?

Now set your goals for the next three months.

Yearly goals

What do you intend to have achieved in your leisure activities by this time next year?

- Active membership of an organisation (e.g. a swimming club or a football team)?
- One or more new activities?
- A more *balanced* approach to leisure and recreation?
- Anything else?

Now set your overall leisure/recreation goals for the next year.

Personal Development

These goals are closely linked to leisure/recreation goals, but they are not necessarily the same.

Three-monthly goals

- Review your skills, hobbies and interests.
- Do you play a musical instrument?
- Do you draw, paint or have an interest in any other form of art?
- Are you interested in drama, science, debating or any other kind of clubs?
- Do you take part in any sports?
- Do you have a part-time job?

- Are you interested in any kind of community work?
- Are you politically active; are you involved in any organisation such as Amnesty International or International Aid?
- Are there any issues such as confidence/self-belief/ability to communicate that you feel you need to work on?

Now set your goals for the next three months.

Yearly goals

What do you intend to have achieved in your personal development by this time next year?

- Skill/performance at a particular level in your chosen activities?
- Confidence gained by, for example, taking on a part-time job, dealing with members of the public, active involvement in an organisation, using Information Technology, dramatic activities . . . ? (The possibilities for personal development are endless.)

Now set your overall personal development goals for the next year.

Relationships
Three-monthly goals

- Review your personal relationships.
- How are you getting along with your: *parents,*

grandparents, brothers/sisters, other relatives?
- How are things at school with your: *teachers, fellow students?*
- How do you treat your friends? How do they treat you?
- How do you treat your boyfriend/girlfriend if you have one?
- How do you treat members of the public?

Now set your goals for the next three months.

Yearly goals

What do you intend to have achieved in your relationships by this time next year?
- Re-establish good relationships with particular individuals?
- Improve your relationships with parents, friends or whoever?
- If you know that a particular relationship is harmful to you, you may aim to *improve* it, or *end* it if that's more appropriate.

Now set your overall relationship goals for the next year.

Spiritual Development
Three-monthly goals
- Review your spiritual ideals.
- If you are a religious person, do you follow the instructions/guidelines of your faith?

- If you are not religious in the formal sense, have you developed a code that encourages *respect for self, respect for others, respect for the world*?
- Do you need to do some thinking or research to help settle doubts or to help you formulate a moral code?

Yearly goals

What do you intend to have achieved in your spiritual development by this time next year?

- Active participation in your religion?
- Completion of a course in ethics, morality or suchlike?
- A greater awareness of higher ideals?
- Anything else?

Now set your overall spiritual development goals for the next year.

Career

Three-monthly goals

- Review any career goals.
- What do you need to do to develop your career goals?
  For example: *gain more information,*
   learn how to write an effective CV,
   do some research into training courses,
   gain experience through part-time work.
- If you have no career goals yet, are you thinking about, and developing, your talents and interests? (Rest

assured these will lead you on to the right path.)
- Are there any other questions about your career you can think of?

Now set your goals for the next three months.

Yearly goals

Where do you hope to be on your career path by this time next year?
- One stage nearer college or training?
- Actually in college or on a training programme?
- More aware of your likes/dislikes, your strengths/weaknesses so that you will be nearer the point where you can make an informed choice?
- Anything else?

Now set your overall goals for the next year.

By regularly setting, reviewing and amending your goals you will provide yourself with a *focus* that will always keep you on the direction that is best for you.

Having a sense of direction and purpose is more than just a luxury: it is an essential ingredient in successful living. Some people have a narrow view of success, thinking of it only as the ability to run a business or make lots of money. But success is more than that: it is the achievement of goals that help develop your potential. This may be in commerce, in sport, in community service, in education – in whatever area your particular interest lies. You may see success as achieving personal fulfilment, such as learning to accept circumstances that you can't change, but changing those which you can.

Cheryl, Louise – and a night they won't forget!

The most important thing is to have a sense of **focus**. One Monday morning last year two students, Cheryl and Louise, came in to school beaming with pleasure. They'd spent their Friday night and most of Saturday morning lining up to buy tickets for their favourite band. The Friday night had been a pretty harsh affair! It was well into the winter months and a cold, driving rain had been blowing down from the north. Undaunted, the two girls had armed themselves with warm flasks, as many clothes as they could wear and a few blankets. Then they joined the other die-hards in the queue to be sure of their tickets when the box-office opened on Saturday. Can you imagine spending the night in the open during the winter? Most people would last one hour at the most before heading for their home comforts! What was it that kept these girls going hour after freezing hour? Obviously it was the prospect of seeing and hearing their favourite band in a live concert. Although they were cold, wet, tired and hungry, they knew as they approached the box-office next morning that they were reaching their goal, and it was *that focus* that enabled them to stay in line overnight.

SETTING **GOALS**

Now try to imagine this scene. Supposing after their overnight ordeal the two girls approached the box-office and said:

'Two tickets, please.'
'OK. Which concert?'
'Oh, any one, it doesn't matter . . .'
'But you must have some idea . . .'
'Well . . . no. We've no idea what gigs are coming up. Just give us anything you have.'
'Right. How much would you like to pay?'
'Em . . . don't know. We haven't really thought about it.'

Ludicrous, isn't it? Nobody would have the *motivation* to line up overnight unless they had a very clear idea of what they wanted. Yet many people go through *life* without any clear idea of what they want. And when times get rough they cave in because they have no sense of purpose to keep them going. You can accept for sure that life will present you with some major challenges. There's no comparison between Nelson Mandela's challenges and the challenges facing Cheryl and Louise lining up for their tickets. But what they had in common was a clear goal that sustained them through the hard times. The Scout Association has a motto: 'Be prepared'.

If you haven't already started, why not start now?

> **SMART TIPS**
>
> *1 Set yourself three-monthly goals and yearly goals for all the major areas of your life.*
>
> *2 Review these goals regularly, updating them when necessary. See how you have been tackling them, and how successful your approach has been or how you can improve it.*
>
> *3 Start now!*

Chapter 9

Live Your Dreams

In March 1999, a British dad named Brian Jones was flying high. He and his Swiss co-pilot, Bertrand Picard, had just completed a record-breaking, round-the-world flight in a balloon. The flight of 74,814 kilometres had taken ninteen days, twenty-one hours and fifty-five minutes!

They had started from the Swiss Alps, but it wasn't long before they met a whole series of challenges: the burners played up and had to be repaired; icicles formed on the balloon, slowing them and wasting their fuel; there was more ice over the mountains; there were storms over the Pacific; there were political problems about airspace; the heating in the capsule broke down; then when they landed in an Egyptian desert at the end of their trip they had to spend eight hours in the searing heat before being picked up. When asked, Bertrand described everything as 'Absolutely wonderful'!

They had, after all, set a new world record and they had achieved a goal they'd been working towards for years. The men dedicated their achievement to the children of the world, saying:

'Our achievement shows the value of dreams.'

Brian's wife, Joanna, backed up this belief:

'This makes you realise dreams can come true for ordinary people.'

This story appeared on 21 March, 1999. Yet on the same day the press published the results of a survey which showed that eighty-eight per cent of young people in Britain were more stressed about their school performance than anything else. Two-thirds described themselves as 'worriers' and about half claimed to have lost sleep over concern about exams.

Believe it or not, *dreaming* can help with this. The type of dreaming Jones and Picard were referring to is not simply daydreaming (which can be enjoyable and relaxing in its own right); nor is it just *wishing for something*. No, it means constantly keeping your mind focused on your goal to the point where you can imagine it's actually happening here and now. This is an extension of the positive affirmations and it can be intensified during relaxation.

Dreaming And The Future

Here's a suggestion for constructive dreaming.

1 Review your goals and select the one you want to 'dream' about.

2 Now RELAX so that your mind can go into a **suggestible** state. Get comfortable and make sure you're in a quiet place where you won't be disturbed. Sit or lie down (but if you become too comfortable you may fall asleep!).

3 If you can, listen to some quiet, relaxing music, preferably through headphones to cut down outside noise. (Music is helpful in relaxation, but it's not essential.)

4 Slow down your breathing and take deeper breaths. Empty your lungs by breathing out and at the same time press gently on your diaphragm (just below your chest and above your abdomen). As you breathe in, slowly and deeply through your nose, you should feel this area rising, then sinking again as you breathe out through your mouth. Do this a few times until you're satisfied that your breathing is slower, deeper and more rhythmic than usual.

5 Now *tell* yourself to relax the main parts of your body. For example, you could say:

> *Relax your feet.*
>
> (Have a short pause between commands.)
>
> *Relax your ankles.*

SMART THINKING

Relax your calves.
Relax your thighs.
Relax your hips.
Relax your lower back and abdomen.
Relax your upper back and chest.
Relax your shoulders.
Relax your arms all the way to your elbows,
  all the way to your wrists,
  and all the way to your fingertips.
Relax your neck.
Relax your jaw, your eyes and your forehead.

Take a deep breath, and as you slowly let it out, feel a tingling sensation run all the way down your body from the top of your head to the tips of your toes. (Note the constant repetition of the word 'relax'. This also sounds as if someone else is talking to you, and this helps your subconscious to be more open to suggestion. Some people make up a tape with music and a voice-over talking them through the commands.)

6 If you are playing relaxing music, at this point you could spend a few moments just listening and allowing your imagination to go where the music takes you.

7 You're now in a state of mental and physical relaxation. Your mind is now more receptive, so visualise your goal.

8 See and hear things not in the future but *as if they are happening now and as if you achieved your goal*.

9 Try to *intensify* your vision. Bring the full range of the senses into your imagination. (We know that Muhammad Ali used to visualise what he called his 'future history'. He didn't say, 'I'm going to win my next fight'. He tells us he used to project his mind to the point where *the fight had been won*. He would 'hear' the crowd, he would 'feel' himself being carried aloft, he would 'smell' the ring, and he would 'see' and 'feel' the massive winner's belt round his waist. And it all came true.)

10 Now use your spiritual beliefs. Give your plans over to the higher, positive power you believe in. You will either achieve that dream, or if the dream wasn't in your best interests you will come to realise why, and you will achieve something equally spectacular.

11 You're now ready to bring yourself back to a normal, wakeful state; but if you're doing this last thing at night you may want to drift off into a peaceful sleep. The positive images you've created will remain with you. If, however, you're coming back to normal it's a good idea to count slowly to ten as, no matter how lively you feel, your blood pressure may have dropped very slightly and it doesn't like to be rushed! The techniques of relaxation are entirely natural and beneficial and as a society we're beginning to appreciate how much we've suffered by neglecting them.

Bear in mind, too, that some students enjoy just using the music and fantasy techniques without always concentrating on their goals. It helps them relax before exams and other potentially stressful activities.

Dreaming and the past

You can use the relaxation sequence for looking *back* as well as looking *forward*. Suppose, for example, you now lack confidence because an adult used to laugh at, or ridicule, your singing or dancing or even your attempts to express your point of view. Your ability to express yourself will have suffered and you'll be carrying pent-up anger or resentment that still hurts!

Resentment is one of the major barriers to personal development. Try to do everything in your power to get rid of it. When you're in your 'dream' state (as described), you can imagine yourself travelling back to the time and place where the damage or hurt was done. Tell yourself that if at any time you feel too distressed you can come out of your sequence *instantly*. (This is like a 'panic button': if it's there you'll feel reassured and will probably never have to use it!)

It will help if you create an image of yourself actually travelling, perhaps in a time machine or along a beam of light. The Right Brain loves bright pictures, remember, and stimulating the imagination in this way will help access the restoring powers of intuition.

It's good to be clear about the purpose of this 'journey'. It's to put matters right, not to get your own back. 'Having a go' at someone may make you feel good, but in the long run it will not remove the difficulty. *Giving in to resentment never does.*

Travel back in your imagination and greet the person in a civil manner. If you feel intimidated, use the technique described earlier to banish your fear and if necessary 'reduce' the image of the person to a non-threatening, cartoon-like character.

Now explain that their actions during your childhood were very hurtful and damaging to your development. Did they realise this, or were they just being tactless and insensitive? Go into the *specific details* of your experience here.

If it becomes obvious that the person never intended the damage and never even realised it had been done, explain that it did cause you a lot of unhappiness. At the end, however, stress that you *forgive* them and that you're no longer going to allow the damage or hurt to continue. (You may have to have a few sessions like this to get it all off your chest.) But tell them you'll accept an apology and you will turn the experience into a positive one.

How should you respond if it becomes obvious that it was a calculated attempt to hurt or humiliate you? Admit that, yes, they succeeded but you *pity* anyone who feels the need to treat a child in that way. Say that although the past cannot *literally* be relived, you are now in control of your response and you're not allowing the hurt to continue. You're now leaving all feelings of fear, hurt, anger and resentment in the past where they will drift away in the mists of time.

When you return from your imaginary journey you will not only have cast off the burden of the past, you will have turned it to your advantage: you'll now be a more understanding and sensitive person.

You may discover elsewhere a relaxation sequence that suits you better, or you may adapt different ideas and come up with a formula of your own. It's the same as with all such exercises:

The key to success is practice.

Another useful technique is 'mental rehearsal' of events just before they actually happen (as distinct from during your private relaxation sessions). 'See' yourself:
- passing that exam;
- winning that race;
- giving that performance of a lifetime;
- helping those children;
- assisting those elderly or sick people.

Then, when the time comes, it's as if you've done it all before!

SMART TIPS

1 Dream about your goals! Get into a state of relaxation (see pages 97–9), and envelop yourself in a detailed image of your success. Use it to focus and motivate yourself.

2 Use the relaxation techniques to dream about the past too. Revisit incidents that still bother you: acknowledge your emotions, then let go of the negative feelings, such as anger or resentment.

Chapter 10

Assertiveness Rules!

Facing up to intimidating situations in your past is a form of assertiveness, but if you really want to 'be more' you need to assert yourself effectively in your everyday life. Some people, however, think they're being **assertive** when they are in fact being **aggressive**.

The Aggressive Person

Let's examine the characteristics of the aggressive person. They tend to thrust themselves forward and adopt an 'in your face' attitude. Often their eyes look on fire, the face is flushed, the voice is loud and harsh, and their language is offensive. They tend to repeat themselves and just don't listen to the other person's point of view. They can easily lose control – and often friends!

This usually goes hand-in-hand with low self-esteem, as the aggressors see themselves as unable to match up to others and they lack the skills of putting their views calmly and assertively. They haven't learned the skills of *courtesy* and *listening*, and they copy the aggressive behaviour of the role models in their lives. We've all heard of aggressive families known as 'the neighbours from hell'!

The Passive Person

At the opposite end of the scale is a type of behaviour that is equally to be avoided. The *passive* person is like a puppet that relies on someone else to pull its strings. He or she will keep the peace at any cost, rarely raising a voice in protest even when their own rights are involved. Instead of thrusting themselves forward (like the aggressors) they tend to hang back, often hovering around, trying to pluck up the courage to speak. And when they do they are timid, speaking nervously and quietly. They avoid eye contact, keeping the head and eyes down.

As a means of gaining approval, the passive person is often too eager to please. Simon, who spoke earlier about his life at boarding school, remembers one such boy:

After meals at school there was a work session and every student had to take his turn at household chores, like clearing the tables or sweeping the floors. You could switch with someone else, just as long as the duty was covered. There was one boy who was so passive he just couldn't say 'No'. Boys used to ask him to stand in for them, then they would conveniently 'forget' to repay the favour. As a result this boy was on work duty almost every day. He would never complain. Someone only had to approach him and he would meekly give in. Eventually the housemaster got to know about this and there was hell to pay. Significantly, it wasn't the boy himself who reported the matter. But everybody recognised that they'd been taking advantage of him, so his life began to improve: he wasn't bullied and no one asked him to do extra duties again. I left the school about fifteen months later, so I don't know how his life has turned out. I hope he has learned to hold his own with others, because he no longer has the housemaster around!

How many young people today are involved in such things as drugs, shoplifting, or skipping school, not because they actively decide on such actions themselves, but because they passively go along with others? They just haven't developed the ability to decide for themselves and stand up to others.

During the 1980s in the USA, there was an anti-drugs campaign with the slogan: *Just say, 'No!'* At school, in the disco, or in a club, if anyone tried to push drugs in your direction all you had to do was say no and walk away. The campaign was well-intentioned but it failed. This was probably because it never recognised the power of group pressure. As you know very well, it can be the hardest thing in the world to stand up against the group. Relatively few young people are aggressive, but many more are passive. The don't want to incur the ridicule of their friends, so even when they know it's wrong, they'll go along with the crowd. Sometimes this 'herd mentality' can be a great advantage and it can support us through our challenges. At other times it can be utterly destructive. The weakness in the *Just say 'No!'* slogan lay in the word 'Just'. It suggested that saying no was easy! Standing up against your friends or the crowd demands the skills of confidence, self-assurance and assertiveness. You really have to be *strong*.

The Assertive Person

Assertive people may not welcome negative responses like ridicule and anger being hurled at them, but they know they can handle it and they're prepared to speak up. They remain calm and in control. In their approach to others they stand up confidently. They look other people squarely in the eye and hold eye contact easily. Their voices are audible, well-paced and their comments and opinions are clearly expressed. They refuse to let others intimidate them.

Assertiveness opens many doors and will lead to a more contented, relaxed and healthy lifestyle. Contrast this with the aggressive person's soaring blood pressure, or the passive person's seething frustration! There's yet another benefit from assertiveness, a spin-off if you like . . .

Emotional Awareness

Being assertive will help you to recognise and understand emotions in yourself and others. Aggressive people go around in an emotional turmoil. If their response is always *attack! attack*!, then they rarely stop to think. Eventually they don't even recognise what's going on in their heads, as they're at the beck and call of their **reptilian brain**. Highly passive people are usually so angry with themselves that they soon suffer from self-loathing; they, too, tend to live in an *emotional* rather than a *rational* state.

Assertive people, however, are confident, calm and secure in their own identities. By dealing positively with their thoughts and feelings, they are in a better position to observe and understand just what is going on in their minds and the minds of others.

Tips For Becoming Assertive

All the exercises mentioned earlier will help you to develop assertiveness!

- Slow, deep and regular breathing is VITAL. Remember what was said about remaining in control.
- Work on those positive affirmations; they *will* pay off!
- Push back that Comfort Zone. Confidence in one area can be transferred to another – and every time you try to be assertive you are stepping out of your normal zone.

ASSERTIVENESS RULES!

- Use your Right Brain to create comfortable images so that you can assert yourself with ease. The more ridiculous, bizarre or funny you 'see' a threatening situation the better!
- Regularly practise mental rehearsals of events – and that includes occasions when you have to assert yourself with 'difficult' people.
- Work on your **body language**: observe and *learn* the characteristics of assertive people (body held erect, eye contact maintained, voice audible, etc, as previously described). Practise them in 'comfortable' situations – then use them when you need to be assertive!
- Practise the techniques of assertiveness with your friends. Remember not to take yourselves too seriously – and laugh!

As always, practice is the key to success. If you *really* find being assertive a challenge, you could attend one of the many classes that are available nowadays. If your school doesn't run one, then it's almost certain there will be an evening or weekend class in your local area.

If you're not **assertive**, you will be either **aggressive** or **passive**. Can you afford to live your life like that?

SMART TIPS

1 Practise assertiveness. Look at yourself and recognise passive and aggressive behaviour.

2 Use the tips for becoming assertive given on pages 108–9.

3 Assertiveness isn't always easy, but it becomes easier with practice. Be calm and confident. Keep working at it: it'll make you feel empowered and you'll get the best out of situations and relationships.

Chapter 11

Half-empty Or Half-full?

An **optimist** is someone who looks on the bright side, while a **pessimist** always looks on the bleak side. If your friend offered you half a bottle of your favourite drink, would you be pleased because it was half-full or disappointed because it was half-empty? In reality it is *both*, but the person who is pleased and thinks of it as half-full is going to enjoy it more! Being optimistic brings more rewards.

If you train yourself to see the *good* things in a situation, then you will be programming your subconscious mind to constantly seek out a solution when the chips are down. The negative person, on the other hand, will focus only on the 'problem' and will be hard-pressed to come up with an answer. So even when everything is going your way it pays to make an extra effort to be enthusiastic, outgoing and cheerful. That way, when the challenges appear, your response to them will be automatic.

Being Proactive

How do you react to new situations? Do you strive to be **proactive** at all times? This means you will take action to *direct* the circumstances of your life, rather than have to *respond* to events when they occur.

How do you react when new students come to your school?

Do you treat them with indifference, or shyly keep out of their way? Or do you make a point of welcoming them with enthusiasm and confidence?

How about new teachers?

Do you hanker after the teacher you used to have, the one who understood you so well, and do you decide things can never be as good again? Or do you welcome the new teacher as someone who can bring a different style, a new perspective on things that can challenge and develop you further?

How about new courses and new subjects?

Are these things to be feared because they might be 'difficult', or are they opportunities to learn new and useful things?

New equipment?

Ryan, a school student, once boasted that as far as computers were concerned, he was proud to consider himself useless.

HALF-EMPTY OR **HALF-FULL**?

His one and only passion at school was physical education (PE). And in this he excelled! Games, athletics, circuit training – you name it, Ryan was far and away the best. Even the lessons on theory interested him and he always gained high grades. Then in his final year it nearly all came unstuck. As part of the assessment process for the certificate, students had to submit a detailed investigation on a chosen aspect of their work in PE. Ryan, of course, had so many possibilities that he was spoiled for choice. *Yet the whole process was a major ordeal as he lacked even the most basic word-processing skills.* Handwritten reports were simply not acceptable – and investigations were expected to include diagrams, columns of data, appendices and so on. To gain his certificate Ryan had to learn, and learn fast, to use a computer! He did it, and he learned a valuable lesson at the same time: a more positive attitude to new equipment earlier in his career could have made all the difference!

There are few certainties in life, but we can be sure of these two:

1 The past is gone.
2 Change is inevitable.

So why not welcome change as a new adventure, a new opportunity to develop your potential? Take the action you need to take as soon as the opportunity arises.

Many students think they have to be 'in the mood' before doing something creative like writing, drawing or composing music. But human nature is such that if we waited until the mood came upon us we would rarely attempt anything! Inspiration is not like lightning; it rarely strikes, not even the most gifted. Musicians, artists and writers the world over tell us that they don't wait until the spirit moves them. They have to get down to work whether they feel like it or not, and move the spirit! *It's when you've made that positive step and got underway that creativity will blossom.*

There's also a physical dimension to this. You're more likely to feel positive about new people and new situations if you feel good about yourself. As you go about your life you can make yourself feel *special* or *on top* or *relaxed* or however you want to, by the way you dress and present yourself.

Marie's Story

An American colleague tells the story of a very cruel joke played on a high school girl, Marie, who was, to put it mildly, rather plain. Her hair was lank and in poor condition, her complexion could have been clearer, and she had very little, if any, skill with make-up. She was rather overweight and her dress sense was unflattering. At the beginning of the semester some boys decided they would make fun of her by constantly paying her compliments. They would

HALF-EMPTY OR **HALF-FULL?**

pass by and one would say, 'Nice dress, Marie!' Later it would be, 'Great hair-do!' and the rest would snigger behind her back. Over the term the phoney compliments continued: 'Cool sweater!', 'Wow, you're lookin' good, Marie!' – while the others stuck their fingers down their throats as if being sick. As the year went on they teased Marie about which lucky guy she would invite to the prom. She even had a chance, they told her, of being voted Homecoming Queen.

There was just one snag. Marie never ever knew they were mocking her. She never saw the antics behind her back; she took their compliments at face value!

And a subtle change took place.

Over the months the 'positive' feedback paid off. Thinking she was the centre of attraction, Marie began to take an interest in herself. She lost some weight, took more care over her hair, learned how to apply make-up effectively, and gained the confidence to be more adventurous with her clothes.

Well, Marie never got to be Homecoming Queen. But for the first time in her life she was an eye-catcher and was in great demand at the prom! The cruel joke had backfired in the nicest possible way . . .

You've probably been told, 'Don't judge by appearances',

yet appearances have such a profound effect on everything we do. The fact is, the way you appear, or *think* you appear, can have a very large bearing on your confidence and, therefore, on your performance.

You Are What You Eat – And Drink!

So much for the way you appear on the outside. How about the way you treat your body on the inside? We know that what goes on in the mind has an effect on the body, *but what goes on in the body also has an effect on the mind*.

Let's take the case of two imaginary students who have the same interests and abilities. They are the same age, in the same class and have the same exams coming at the end of term.

One of them has become quite a heavy smoker and is a keen devotee of under-age drinking. She keeps late hours and has been known to experiment with designer drugs at late-night raves. Often this means she misses classes as she just can't get her head together the morning after. And when she *does* attend, there are days when she can't concentrate for more than a few minutes at a time. Her lifestyle is too busy for her to have regular meals, so she survives on a steady diet of junk food. Heavy make-up helps conceal her blotchy complexion and the bags under her eyes. But part of her *wants* to succeed, so for a few weeks before the exams she crams and crams. She's a bright kid, after all, she can handle it! So for a while the late nights are taken up with her

HALF-EMPTY OR **HALF-FULL**?

books and endless cups of coffee to keep her alert.

The other student is by no means a 'Goody Two Shoes', but her lifestyle is quite different. Smoking is out; apart from what it would do to her health, her breath and her hair, she would rather have all that money to spend on what she *chooses*, rather than on what she *needs* to feed an addiction. She enjoys her weekends, meeting friends and going dancing, but alcohol and drugs have never held any attraction for her. She's a keen swimmer and enjoys athletics, so she is fit and energetic. She attends school regularly and concentrates in her classes. She wants to keep her good looks, so she watches her diet; she eats less meat than she used to, she has cut back on sugar, and she's developing a taste for fruit and vegetables. Her regular attendance has meant that she has kept up with her studies, so when the exam period looms on the horizon there's no need for cramming and coffee.

These are two students with similar potential, but which is on line for success?

OK, right now you may be thinking, 'Boring! Give me the life of the first one anytime!' Long live teenage rebellion! But deep down you must know that if it's success you're after, if you want to make the most of your opportunities and talents, then you must be aware of the needs of body, mind and soul. It's a matter of finding the balance between *fun* and *looking after yourself*, the balance that's right for you and helps you to get the most out of your life.

SMART TIPS

1 Be optimistic! You can, by sheer willpower, find the positive in any situation.

2 Act, don't react: direct the circumstances of your life rather than respond to them. Be proactive and take control. It increases confidence and helps overcome fear.

3 Embrace and anticipate change. See it as a challenge, an opportunity for further fulfilment.

4 Don't wait for 'the mood' to do things to hit you: work at it and it'll come.

5 Make yourself feel special! If you value and appreciate yourself, others will see the difference and respond to it. It will change you – your confidence and therefore your performance.

6 Be kind to your body: have healthy food, lots of water, exercise and sleep. If you're healthy and feeling good, it'll have a knock-on effect on your mind and performance.

Chapter 12

Take A Break!

No matter how positive your language, how successfully you challenge your Comfort Zone, how much progress you've made, there's a threat just waiting to worm its way in and send all your advances spinning crazily out of order.

It's fatigue. Yes, ordinary, everyday exhaustion! There's a sign that appears on the motorways:

> **TIREDNESS CAN KILL. TAKE A BREAK.**

This is not just good advice for drivers. Tiredness can cause havoc with students too! Look out for the signs. They can be physical. For example:

- stiffness in the back or the joints;
- a headache, or soreness in the eyes;

- a buzzing in the ears;
- dryness in the throat;
- a lack of energy.

They can also be emotional:

- being irritable and snapping at people;
- having difficulty in concentrating;
- lacking enthusiasm;
- feeling sorry for yourself;
- feeling that you will *never* get things done;
- feeling things are spinning out of control;
- perhaps even feeling misery and despair.

This can come about by working long hours without a proper break, or without enough food or drink. It could be because of a lack of sleep over a sustained period. Or there could be a lack of balance between work and leisure.

Whatever the cause, if you find yourself overtired you should follow the golden rule:

RETREAT!

- Avoid making decisions.
- Don't try to be assertive or to settle an argument.
- Forget reasoning with yourself or others.
- When you're tired your Chatterbox has a great time and

will try to pull you down. Just drop everything and back off! Your positive gains are still intact; it's just that you've allowed yourself to become overtired.

But how can you prevent this happening? By making sure that you always have what is now widely known as QRT: **Quality Recovery Time**. If possible plan your day so that you have a balance between work, leisure and rest.

Notice the distinction between leisure and *rest*. If you've spent long hours on challenging work, you can justifiably feel tired. But the answer may not be to *rest*, in the sense of sitting around and doing nothing, or going straight to bed. Your mind and body may not be able just to switch off. You may need *alternative stimulation*. If you've been working with your brain, why not balance this by trying something physical? Go for a swim, go dancing, meet your friends and catch up with all the latest. That way your brain will calm down and be better prepared for rest.

Guidance counsellors in schools meet many students who have yet to master the art of balancing study and leisure. Too many reach the stage where they try and try – but seem to take nothing in! Assignment deadlines are missed, they fall out with teachers, they dread opening a book and they dread coming to school. They are . . . just . . . so . . . tired . . . Their minds are like vacuum cleaners! When you don't empty the bag in your cleaner the machine goes on trying to suck up dust, but has to work harder and harder to less and less effect. This causes the motor to overheat; but there's a built-in safeguard. The power cuts out to allow the motor to cool down. You won't be able to use the cleaner for some time until the temperature is back to normal. Once it's had its rest – and you've changed the bag! – the vacuum will burst into life and you can get on with the job.

The brain operates along similar lines. You can fill it with information and use its powers of reason and interpretation, but it can only take so much at a time. If you neglect your QRT, then you'll stuff your head with too much and, just as with the vacuum cleaner, the safety switch will kick in. It's as if the brain goes into shut-down; it wants a rest before you push it to breakdown! Many students – and their parents – don't understand this, so they think the answer is to work harder. They try their chemistry assignments, their maths equations, their English essays – but they may just as well be staring at a blank page.

The need for QRT in a balanced study/leisure/rest programme is one that really needs to be appreciated. With a rest period and a new approach to their studies these students make a quick recovery, but at what cost in terms of nervous energy, anxiety, frustration and often despair . . . ?

So if you're overcome by fatigue, keep calm and promise yourself a good rest at the earliest opportunity. All will be well – but only after that rest!

SMART TIPS

1 Don't overdo it! Tiredness and stress sap energy and positivity and make it harder to deal with things and achieve success.

2 Have fun! You'll find confidence and success come more easily and naturally.

3 Give yourself space. Step back from things and allow yourself to rest and relax.

4 Try for balance. If you're using your brain a lot, do something physical. If you're always busy, try doing nothing for a while!

Chapter 13

And Finally!

The main point to take from all this is:

You can raise your level of achievement to whatever level YOU DECIDE – regardless of what it is at present.

It's a well-known fact that many able children give the *opposite* impression at school and are under-achievers. Perhaps they're just on a different wavelength and nobody understands them. Think of Thomas Edison, who gave us so many things we rely on today. (Not just the light bulb!) He was expelled from school for being a slow learner.

So let's return full circle:

IT'S ALL ABOUT BELIEF!

Constant exposure to positive inputs will help you to develop this magic ingredient. Read books and listen to tapes that will fill your life with creative, positive and dynamic messages.

AND **FINALLY**!

To replace old and destructive thought-patterns with new, constructive ones you must stick with your creative visualising and positive affirmations. The success of these depends on three things: REPETITION, REPETITION and – **REPETITION**!

You've been given a set of tools. You must now do the work with them. You have invested in this book, so read it over and over until the ideas become second nature. Putting these ideas into practice is what's really meant by smart thinking. Try it, and you will definitely **be more** – more confident, happy, successful – whatever *you* decide. The list is endless.

Have a fantastic life!

INDEX

aggression 104–5, 107, 108
assertiveness 104–10
attitudes, 68–71, 80

belief 8–15, 57, 68, 124
body language 109
brain (the) 11–12, 58–65, 67, 108, 109, 122

careers 10, 84, 90–1
change 112–13, 118 (see also 'Comfort Zone')
college (see under 'school')
Comfort Zone 37–48, 75, 86, 108, 119
confidence 9, 10, 17, 37–48, 88, 100, 107, 108, 110, 116, 118
creativity 64–7, 77, 109, 114

depression 10
dreams 96–103

emotional awareness 108

failure 11
fear 11, 41–4, 48, 49, 52–7, 60–1, 67, 118
friends 12

goals 81–94, 96, 98

health 116–18
humour 62–4, 66, 67, 77, 80, 109

inner child (the) 74–5

jobs (see under 'careers')

laughter (see under 'humour')
leisure activities 86–8, 121–3

optimism (see under 'positivity')

parents 10, 13
passivity 105–7, 108
peer pressure 12, 106–7
positive affirmations 71–9, 80, 81–2, 96, 108, 125
positive language 18, 28–35, 36
positivity 17–18, 26, 111–18
potential 11, 12, 13
pressure 10–11, 12

relationships 88–9
relaxation 96–100, 103
repression 52–6
repetition 78–9, 80, 109, 125

school 10, 12–13, 52, 85–6, 96, 105–6, 116–17, 120–3
self-esteem 10, 57
self-image 22
spiritual wellbeing 89–90
stress 10, 60
studies (see under 'work')
subconscious (the) 19–20, 49, 68, 78, 82, 98, 111
success 10, 11, 12–13, 91–2, 117
suggestibility 20, 49, 97

tiredness 116–17, 119–23

trauma 49–50, 52–7

visualisation 23, 26, 65, 98, 125 (see also 'dreams')

work 10, 11, 84–6

If you would like more information about books available from Piccadilly Press and how to order them, please contact us at:

Piccadilly Press Ltd.
5 Castle Road
London
NW1 8PR

Tel: 020 7267 4492
Fax: 020 7267 4493

Feel free to visit our website at
www.piccadillypress.co.uk